THE *Ribbon* IN HER JOURNAL

ABCDEFGHIJK
LMNOPQRSTU
VWXYZ 1995
Newport Rhode Island

THE *Ribbon* IN HER JOURNAL

A TRIBUTE TO THE LIFE AND LEGACY OF

Phyllis Hoffman DePiano

BRIAN HART HOFFMAN AND ERIC HOFFMAN

83 press

We dedicate this book to the woman who wrote it, our mom,

PHYLLIS NORTON HOFFMAN DEPIANO.

Her words guide us each and every day.

This is the memoir that she never got to finish—

we hope to make you proud, Mom. We miss you so much!

In memory of our hero.

October 17, 1953–July 10, 2023

"I hope that we all are making wonderful memories for those we love."

Phyllis

CONTENTS

Hoffman Media
2323 2nd Avenue North
Birmingham, AL 35203
hoffmanmedia.com

ISBN # 979-8-9899185-6-0
Printed in USA

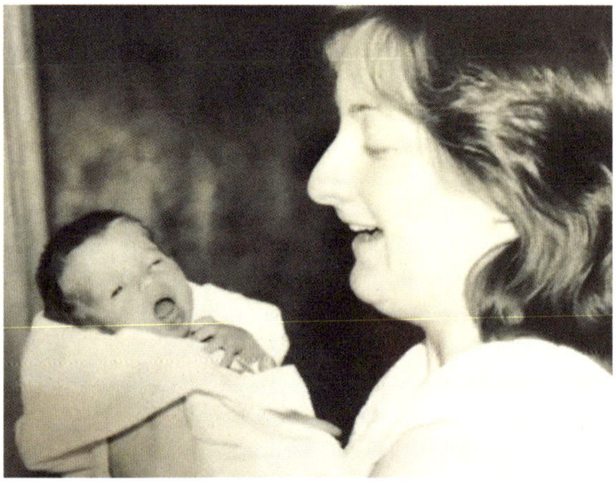

12 O'CLOCK
6 O'CLOCK
give a quarter turn
–Brian Hart Hoffman

INTRODUCTION BY BRIAN HART HOFFMAN

PHYLLIS HOFFMAN DEPIANO IS A NAME that means a lot to many people, but to me and my twin brother, Eric, she was Mom. More than Mom, she was also my hero, mentor, boss, and best friend. Phyllis's time with us came to an end on July 10, 2023, and my heart was forever changed. I move forward with a huge hole that can't be filled—but it can be the reminder to celebrate her legacy and passions every day—and that is exactly why this book is being published.

In the words she wrote on her blog, *The Ribbon in My Journal*, she didn't want to be remembered for her résumé and professional accolades. "It's not about accomplishments or wealth; it's about loving unconditionally, encouraging others, reaching out a hand to those in need, praying for and with friends who are hurting, and being an example of living our lives in such a way that our family and friends know we are always there for them," wrote Phyllis. But I want you to know more about her professional life so you can better understand the woman we are honoring in this book.

After becoming a CPA in the 1970s and marrying my dad later that decade, she left the professional world to fulfill her biggest dream in life—becoming a mom. She prayed for twins, and in 1981, Eric and I got the best mother in the world, lucky us! During the season of her life away from working, she learned how to cross-stitch from her neighbor and best friend, Barbara Cockerham, adding one more talent to the list that already included sewing and playing the piano and organ. This creative prowess led her, along with her sister, Janice, her best friend, Barbara, and another friend to start a magazine (with zero experience in the space!) called *Just CrossStitch* in 1983. That magazine went on to be the largest needlework magazine in the world, and lots of accolades came with that kind of impact. I will never forget our dad taking Eric and me to an industry trade show in Charlotte, North Carolina, to surprise her after she received a lifetime achievement award. I remember thinking, "Wow, our mom really is something special to so many. I'm so glad she is mine."

Over time, the business went through change and growth and was sold to a larger craft company in 1992 that took the brand—and Mom—to a bigger level. Under the company's ownership, she started *McCall's Quilting* and other brands that aligned with her talents and passions. In 1998, the company was ready for other moves and wanted to relocate the Birmingham, Alabama, operation to Golden, Colorado. But as I told you, being a mom was her dream in life, so she wasn't about to take professional advancement and move my brother and me across the country to a new school for our senior year in high school. She and my dad took out a second mortgage on their home so she could purchase the brands she'd sold. That purchase reincorporated the business as Hoffman Media, and we stayed in Birmingham. I wish the 17-year-old me knew the sacrifice and dedication that required, but that is the woman she was. She never looked back with regret.

In the years that followed, Mom expanded the company's offerings into Southern lifestyle brands, including *Southern Lady*, *Taste of the South*, *Southern Home*, and

Cooking with Paula Deen, as well as other titles dedicated to her passions, like *TeaTime*, *Classic Sewing*, and her blog, *The Ribbon in My Journal*.

But to know the "real" Phyllis, we need only to look back at her life to see her creativity was on display, ever expanding, and there wasn't much that she couldn't do. She and her sister, Janice, learned to sew from their mom, Inez. My mom carried that talent through her life as she went on to make wedding dresses for her niece, Beth, and her daughter-in-law, Katie, and a multitude of dresses for her granddaughter, Amelia, in addition to many other garments for family and friends. Phyllis was a natural when learning to play the piano, so much so that she was playing music by ear and got caught red-handed when her teacher walked over to her at the piano and noticed the sheet music was upside down. She went on to become the pianist at her church at the age of 12 and then she taught herself how to play the organ—using her talent to worship and share the gift of song with those she loved. She recorded four albums—one for Christmas, hymns to honor her parents, and one for Eric's and my weddings. I will never hear piano and organ music without thinking about her. I often play her albums to spend a few "moments with Mom," and I especially feel that connection when I hear her play "Wind Beneath My Wings." Even in her 40s, she kept adding talents to her roster with a paintbrush and canvas. Most people would never be able to share their first painting with the world due to a learning curve and not-so-perfect skill, but not Phyllis. She shared a beautiful garden with an arbor covered in flowers. The painting came from her soul and is absolutely perfect. We are so fortunate to have the tangible products of her talents to remember her by and to surround ourselves with when we need to feel close to her.

I am a "mama's boy." I always have been one, often asking her if I was her favorite. The answer was always, "No, I love both of my boys equally. You're both so different, so there is so much to love!" My reply was always something centered around telling her that she was my favorite mom . . . my only but still so deserving of the praise.

Seventeen years ago, and six months apart, Eric and I left our careers—him on Wall Street, and me as a flight attendant—to join our mom in business. After going five years without a paycheck and working a second job to keep the company afloat and make sure her employees still received paychecks, Phyllis saw the company experiencing growth. She needed help. Her first thought was to ask Eric and me if we had an interest in the company being generational or if she needed to look for other plans to grow and prepare the company to be sold at her retirement. Eric and I both took a leap of faith (here we go, following her example!) and gave up careers we loved only to discover careers we loved even more. And we got to do it alongside our mom.

For the first seven years at the company, I learned and worked in event and brand management and eventually became the chief creative officer. Then, my "Phyllis instinct" kicked in. I was a passionate home baker, and I thought, "Why isn't there a culinary magazine all about baking?" I couldn't wait to tell Mom about my idea and the well-thought-out plan that Brooke Bell, now chief content officer, and I had scribbled in a notepad, only to hear that she wasn't so sure this was going to work. But being Mom and entrepreneur, she agreed to produce a test issue of this new magazine. In the autumn of 2015, the first issue of *Bake from Scratch* hit the newsstands. That issue sold so well that our newsstand team instantly asked if a second issue was on the way. Mom was so proud. The following year, at the min (Magazine Industry News) Awards for the Hottest 30 Launches of the previous year, she was honored as the Publisher of the Year for the launch of *Classic Sewing*; Eric accepted an award for another new launch, *Southern Cast Iron*, that fires his passion for savory cooking; and *Bake from Scratch* won for the Hottest Launch of the Year. Talk about a full circle flashback moment for me when I joined Mom and my brother on the stage to receive an award for our career achievements. Mom's lifetime achievement award from years back was way too soon, because in her lifetime, the achievements never stopped.

You will also read about my first cake baking experience in this book, so maybe, my talents were also on display—or wanting to be—but you'll have to read that story for the full details.

It has been an honor to be able to share my love for baking by showing love to Mom. She often talked about the birthday cake of her childhood, a Cherry-Pecan Cake from Pizitz Bakery, but was never able to find the recipe. For Mother's Day in 2023, I was able to recreate the recipe from her memory. She joined me for tastings so I could tap into her taste memory as the recipe was brought back to life. Little did we know that would be the last Mother's Day I got to spend with her. I'm so glad I have the recipe in my collection, so I can bake the special cake in her honor. I'm sharing that recipe with you, too, along with some others that were special to Mom.

Baking also found its way into Mom's home with her husband, Neal, the love of her life. In her last year, she enjoyed her favorite pound cake, Jo's Whipping Cream Pound Cake, with regularity as Neal mastered baking it to ensure she was always surrounded by her favorite things. Their love and life together brought her so much happiness and inspired a lot of things she shared on her blog. They lived each day as an adventure together, and she even rode on the back of a Harley-Davidson—only with Neal.

My mom's successes weren't her goal, and they didn't define her. They allowed her to be a benevolent gift-giver to so many. Since her passing, we have learned of things she did (sometimes anonymously) to make other's lives better. That is how I want to live my life, too, ensuring that others succeed, feel love, and make it through tough times. Even if you don't have the financial resources, it doesn't mean you can't make a difference. May we all continue to honor Mom's life and legacy by encouraging others, sharing in our successes, and being a beacon of love.

In a full circle of reflection, Mom used to joke with her friends that her kids wouldn't want any of the "stuff" she collected, but in reality, we do. It is only when someone is gone that we cherish the things that remind us most of them. But as I have gotten older, I am just like Mom. I collect antique French copper, culinary items, and "things" as I find them. I now know exactly where that came from. She taught me how to make biscuits in "the biscuit bowl," and I am so grateful that she passed hers on to me many years ago so that we could enjoy time together in the kitchen. I think of her each time I use it and know that her touch is just a memory away.

She always told me that I could do tough things, and writing this has been one of them, but it's an honor to share a sliver of what made Phyllis, my mom, such a spectacular person.

I can, in fact, do tough things. I love you, Mom, and I always will.—*Brian Hart Hoffman, son*

INTRODUCTION BY ERIC HOFFMAN

WHEN I THINK ABOUT MY MOTHER, the late Phyllis Hoffman DePiano, one word repeatedly comes to mind: gratitude. My heart is full of gratitude for so many reasons as I look over the life she lived and the broad impact she had in changing people's lives, including my own. I'm grateful that she was so many things: a loving daughter, a caring mother, a civic leader, a generous giver, an amazing pianist, a committed and faithful person, a risk-taker, a talented entrepreneur and founder.

Describing my mother is a complex task because her passions all intertwined as she lived out each day. Growing up, she was Mom to me in the mornings, when she made breakfast and dropped me off at school; by day, she was CEO of Hoffman Media, driving growth and creativity across the business. In the afternoons and evenings, she was back to Mom, helping with homework and cooking incredible dinners. On Sundays, she was the pianist at church, where she played some of the most beautiful music my ears have ever heard, and she played with heartfelt passion that you could feel. After church, we went to my grandparents' home to enjoy wonderful meals and time together because, to Phyllis, family was most important. But it was not until I was much older that I came to appreciate all the other things she did and who she was.

A tireless and selfless giver, Phyllis never wanted credit. She did many things that I was aware of, such as founding the Auxiliary of Big Oak Ranch, but it was not until her funeral that I learned of so many more things about her that I had never heard before, including her anonymously covering the college education of a student at her church.

Phyllis grew up in Birmingham, Alabama, as the eldest of three children. Her mother, Inez, was an incredible caregiver and homemaker while her father, Oliver, went to work each day. He spent his entire career working for South Central Bell, now AT&T. Her parents taught her about hard work, dedication, living a life of faith, and the importance of giving to others.

Graduating from Shades Valley High School and then earning an accounting degree from the University of Alabama at Birmingham, Phyllis went to work at Ernst & Ernst (now EY) as one of the very first female accountants in the Birmingham office. Her experience at EY further developed her business knowledge while also creating an amazing network of friends and business professionals. She married in 1978, and in support of her husband, moved to Cullman, Alabama, so that he could pursue a career in medicine. In 1981, she gave birth to me and my twin brother, Brian. She put her career on the side to be a mom to twins, who were a handful, no doubt!

While raising infant boys, she took up a new hobby of cross-stitching, learning from her neighbor and friend Barbara Cockerham. It was at that time she came to a pivotal epiphany: there was not a magazine in the cross-stitching industry to help her pursue her passion. In 1983, the family relocated back to Birmingham, and soon after, she started the business Symbol of Excellence Publishers (now Hoffman Media). The company was launched with her sister and two friends, each contributing $500 to the venture, and from the basement of our home, she started creating *Just CrossStitch* magazine. She knew very little about publishing but learned quickly. With assistance from a local printer, the magazine soon came to life.

In the years following, Phyllis came to realize that serving stitching enthusiasts meant so much more than just delivering a magazine, so she launched a catalog that offered prepackaged kits with all the things someone would need to feed their hobby. One of the most incredible moves she made was to go visit The Walt Disney Company and pitch them on licensing all the Disney characters to produce cross-stitching kits. Needless to say, it was a boom and such a big move for a small company. The success she had there allowed her to launch a sister publication and start a consumer event held each year in Williamsburg, Virginia, her favorite city to visit.

In 1992, Phyllis sold her enterprise to PJS Publications, a private-equity-backed enthusiast magazine publisher, and she went to work for them as Group Publisher. When PJS was later sold to PRIMEDIA, because of her gift of vision and leadership, Phyllis was tasked with new magazine launches across several divisions. In 1998, the CEO of PRIMEDIA approached her about moving to Colorado to take on a larger executive role. However, having twin boys in their senior year of high school, she declined. Instead, Phyllis bought back the company she had sold in 1992 and formed what is now Hoffman Media.

Understanding that success depended upon expanding her cross-stitch business, she launched *Southern Lady* magazine in 1999, and it was an instant success. It resonated with women across the South because it was unapologetically Southern and unapologetically for women. The pages of the magazine were filled with wonderful stories and recipes, beautiful tablescapes, and features on women entrepreneurs. She was so passionate about the brand that she launched an event titled Southern Lady Celebration to honor a Southern Lady of the Year. I so wish that she had lived long enough for us to honor her with her very own award, as she was probably more deserving than any.

In 2004, Phyllis would make some strategic moves that set the company on its course today. First, she hired a college friend as the company's first CFO. Soon, they raised private equity to successfully grow the company from $4 million in sales to over $35 million in 2007. Most notably, the success came when Phyllis approached cooking celebrity Paula Deen about launching a magazine. Phyllis had become friends with Paula, as she had been selected as Southern Lady of the Year in 2004, and it was there that Phyllis pitched the idea. In the fall of 2005, *Cooking with Paula Deen* launched, and over the course of just a couple of years, it was arguably the fastest-growing magazine in the US. Phyllis was a risk-taker with such great vision, seeing opportunities others do not see, and she always taught me to follow my gut.

In 2007, I was working in New York as an investment banker after having spent two years at Ernst & Young (which made Mom proud as an EY alum). I got a call from her in February asking if I would be interested in coming home and joining the company as chief operating officer. It was a special moment in my life to accept the job and to come home to partner with my mother to grow Hoffman Media. What I didn't know then was how this step would forever change my life and career, working alongside my mother and learning from her. I was young and had very little experience, but understanding the business side and learning how to run a company were the easier parts. The real lesson in life I learned from her went beyond a boardroom or budgets or profits; simply put, it was that people matter and that the care and concern we share, ultimately, is what we are measured by. This even applies to our millions of readers that we touch each month, as she thought of them all as family. I learned "the why" of our business: to enrich the daily lives of people.

Over the next several years, I saw my mother do some incredible things, including forming a joint venture with Hearst Corporation to relaunch *Victoria* magazine, which had folded in 2003 after 16 years. The brand had perhaps the most passionate base of subscribers I have ever seen, with Phyllis being one herself. To this day, *Victoria* is one of Hoffman Media's largest publications and still has such an amazing group of readers throughout the US, Canada, and even parts of Europe. The other incredible move was bringing on Don Logan, former CEO of Time Inc., as an investor and board member, and he remains so today. He brought a level of expertise like no other and has always been encouraging to all of us through thick and thin.

Through the great recession of 2008–2009, Hoffman Media continued to do well because Phyllis built the business around enthusiasts who were deeply committed to our brands, and they stuck with us. This ultimately set the stage for us to lead a buyout of our private-equity investors in the spring of 2012. Unlike most private-equity deals, our deal resulted in the family, alongside Don Logan, owning the whole thing again rather than selling the company.

In the decade following, the company would develop a path for real transformation, moving into a new headquarters, shifting from predominantly print magazines into several different growth areas, such as consumer events, book publishing with our 83 Press imprint, video production, and e-commerce. In another gut instinct move, Phyllis and our team approached Brenda Gantt about publishing her first cookbook. During the pandemic, Brenda developed a large social media following from her bed-and-breakfast in Andalusia, Alabama, and ultimately agreed to partner with us for a book that was one of the most successful projects we have ever been a part of.

In the months before Mom died, the two of us sat around our conference room table, and I began to share my vision for the business only to be interrupted by her with, "You are ready." It was in that moment she went on to name me CEO. I was speechless. I was humbled because the 40-year journey she led was overwhelming to comprehend, and to know she trusted me in that moment was incredibly moving. I didn't understand until we lost her that, even at the end, she was being Mom. She was making sure that she looked after us, her Hoffman Media family. She always had a plan and didn't leave any business undone.

Losing Mom was one of the hardest days I have ever endured. In the pain and grief that followed, my heart hurt, yet it equally became full of gratitude for the life she lived and who she was to me and to so many. In addition to being one of the most talented people I have ever been around, she was an amazing mom and grandmother, an incredible business leader, a servant to her community, and an inspiration to the world. She leaves such an incredible legacy for us to honor.

—Eric Hoffman, son

Miss Sally Jones
52 Primrose Lane
Mobile, AL
36123

FOREWORD

PHYLLIS HOFFMAN DEPIANO WAS MY DEAR FRIEND, a bright light in my life for more than four decades. We met as neighbors and bonded over our shared love of needlework, traditional architecture and furniture, Colonial Williamsburg, and afternoon tea. She noticed the many counted cross-stitch designs displayed on my kitchen walls when she came to visit and returned the next day with plastic bags filled with fabric, bits of floss, and charts. Little did we know that, within a few years, we would form a company with her sister, Janice, and a friend and would publish a magazine devoted exclusively to cross-stitch, titled *Just CrossStitch*.

In the early days of our friendship, we shared the joys of becoming mothers the same year. My youngest daughter was 3 months old when Phyllis gave birth to twin boys. As we drafted plans for the cross-stitch magazine we produced, those three babies were in carriers near the kitchen table where we worked. My dear friend was multitalented and was multitasking before the word was coined.

Along the way, we expanded our company to include a magazine devoted to the study and preservation of antique cross-stitched samplers, *Sampler & Antique Quarterly*. When we had grown the business and felt the time was right to move on, we sold the publishing company. Five years later, Phyllis bought back the rights to the *Just CrossStitch* title and used it as a springboard to create the broader-based publishing house Hoffman Media.

When Phyllis asked me to join her company, I became one of the many employees who thrived in the creative, fast-paced, and challenging environment. I was honored to be the first editor of *TeaTime* and later to be part of the revival of *Victoria* magazine.

From our first meeting 45 years ago, Phyllis was such a vital part of my life. We worked together for 35 years, as partners at Symbol of Excellence Publishers and later as employer-employee at Hoffman Media until my retirement in 2018. Working with such a dear friend was a privilege indeed. —*Barbara Cockerham, friend and colleague*

Barbara Cockerham

A Journey Begins

When I place a ribbon in my journal, I am marking the place where I stop for the day and where I will begin again tomorrow. Our walk together through this blog, *The Ribbon in My Journal*, will be just that—a journey of celebrating the beautiful things in life one day at a time. It is my hope that when you come here you will find beauty, encouraging words, resources, and inspiration from exciting people who make a difference.

Guest bloggers will talk about their areas of expertise, from cooking to decorating and everything in between. I will be bringing you exciting interviews with wonderful authors, designers, artists, chefs, and other creative people who will inspire us to put our personal touches on everything we do. There are some extraordinary entrepreneurs who turned their hobbies into incredible businesses just like I did years ago. I can't wait to share their stories and mine with you.

We are never too old to keep learning. In fact, the older I get, the more I want to learn. People inspire me, and I hope that you will share the wonderful things going on in your life. There is something special about remembering the momentous or even the simple moments in life.

Sometimes, we just need a few words of encouragement and inspiration to change an otherwise ordinary day into something very special. It is amazing how a few uplifting thoughts can make you look at the world differently. I am looking forward to our walk together. Thank you for joining me.

I'll place my ribbon here, where we will begin next time. *—May 2014*

On the Importance of Family

BABY SISTER

FAMILY WAS OF UTMOST IMPORTANCE to Phyllis, and I was blessed to be her sister. Phyllis was the oldest of the three siblings in our family. Our brother, Keith, was the middle child, and I was the youngest or, as Phyllis always introduced me, "the baby." The three of us were very close in age, and our mother always said we were triplets the hard way! We were fortunate enough to grow up in a home where there was an abundance of love from parents who encouraged us to always try and become the best version of ourselves.

My brother and I were very lucky to have Phyllis as our big sister. She was our protector, our safe place, sometimes our antagonist, and always our loving sister. But we were not the only recipients of Phyllis's love and generosity. In addition to family, Phyllis showered these same gifts to many who called her friend. Friendship was very important to her, and she valued the many special people in her life.

I, along with her family and many friends, miss her every day, but I hold on to the many happy memories that we shared growing up and growing older. She was my sister, my friend, my teacher, and my confidant. I cherish the memories and traditions that we shared together, and I'm so thankful that she wrote about some of these in her blog. The one thing I think Phyllis would say to all of us is to live each day to the fullest and show love to the many special people in your life. *—Janice Ritter, sister*

Janice Ritter

Remembering Granddad

One day, my mom handed me a little cardboard box and told me that I would love what was inside. I had no idea that the contents would delight me as they did. It was a small collection of hand-embroidered postcards that my granddad sent home from France when he was stationed there during WWI.

My dad's father, Oliver Street Norton, bought these pleasant cards to mail home to his mother. Also inside the box was his personal calling card, which is hand-lettered and painted. What a treasure! I have a passion for needlework, but I was astonished that you could buy hand-stitched postcards and mail them. When I studied these, I realized that the fronts of the cards have embroidered designs on silk with tiny stitches that must have taken a great deal of time. I wonder how much he paid for the cards and where he bought them.

My granddad was a farmer who served in the military and returned home after the war to resume his farming life. He was a very quiet man, and when he spoke, you listened. He listened to opera on the radio every Saturday night—very intriguing to me. My grandmother worshipped the ground he walked on, and rightfully so. She was 12 years younger than Granddad, and he had to wait for her to grow up so he could marry her. I have so many memories of their life together on the farm. They grew and picked cotton and made a fun time of it. My favorite memories include sitting in rocking chairs under the shaded canopy of a huge walnut tree in their yard. Conversation was the order of the day.

I wish I had known of this little box back then so I could have asked all the questions about these keepsakes. Isn't that the way it always is? We find these family keepsakes and then wish we had all the details about them. So, I choose to remember my sweet granddad, who bought lovely needlework treasures for his mother, as a man who enjoyed beautiful things in life, from growing cotton to listening to opera.
—August 2014

SOUVENIR FROM FRANCE
M.G.
SOUVENIR

Father's Day and My Dad

When I look back on my childhood, I know my dad probably had the biggest collection of macaroni-crafted pencil holders of any man on the planet. I can't remember if it was school or church where we discovered our macaroni art talent, but all three of us—my sister Janice, my brother Keith, and I—had it!

My favorite pencil holder was an empty orange juice can with glued-on elbow macaroni spray-painted gold. Oh, I was so proud of that creation! I did notice that it stayed on his dresser at home rather than making it to his office at the phone company. I wish I had photos of all the fun things my brother, sister, and I made for him. I loved to make cakes, and I am sure he got his share of Betty Crocker cake mix beauties when I was young. At 90 years old, he still enjoys a good cake or cherry pie. Some things never change.

His name is Oliver Norton, but he was tagged as "Big O" years ago for his great ability to cook the best steaks and grow the best tomatoes. As "Grandad" to six grandchildren and four great-grandchildren, he gleams with pride when they are around and makes everything fun.

My brother and sister and I are lucky to have been raised by him. Dad taught us many things growing up. He taught us how to speak to people, make eye contact, and have good table manners. He also taught us to work hard, as he had done his whole life.

Oliver Norton is the most consistent and disciplined man in the world. He never waivers in his faith, his routine, and working his plans. "Make the plan and work the plan" are his words of advice coupled with Mom's guidance that "you never know if you can do something until you try."

Dad's life IS a life of integrity. If Dad tells you something, you can trust him. You can believe his words and know that he has given a lot of thought before he speaks. His words mean everything, and his handshake is a bond.

He is quite the character and delights in any lighthearted moment. As a retired executive, he now spends time doing what he really loves: gardening. He and Mom have wonderful flower gardens and vegetable gardens. My grandchildren love being in their gardens with him almost as much as I do.

Still singing in the choir at his church, he is loved by so many. Dad is a gentle man and loves unconditionally every one of us lucky enough to be in his family. He cherishes our mom and lets everyone know she is his sweetheart and has been since their high school days.

I love you, Dad, and thank God for you every day. You have modeled for us a life of integrity, consistency, and unconditional love. I am blessed, for there is not really anything else a child needs. This weekend, we celebrate our fathers. Happy Father's Day! —*June 2014*

In 2014, Oliver Norton, a WWII Navy veteran, was honored with the presentation of a US flag that flew over the Alabama Capitol in Montgomery and the city of Hoover, the Birmingham suburb where we live. What a day that was for our family! Everyone was there to support him as Phyllis's husband, Neal, a career fireman, presented Oliver with the neatly folded flag placed inside a triangular case.

—Brian and Eric

A Personal Note on Veterans Day

Since my dad's death, our family has revisited many of the memories and Navy stories he shared about his service during WWII. He and my mom, Inez, were high school sweethearts when he left to serve in the Navy. The written note became so important. They exchanged letters almost every day, and after he read letters from home, they had to be destroyed.

In his memoirs, Dad penned that he wrote Mom a letter and asked her to marry him when he was home on his first leave in 1946. She accepted his proposal by letter, and they were married the Christmas Eve that followed. The proposal and the acceptance—everything was by letter.

Their life together was put on hold while Dad finished his Navy service. Mom and Dad wrote letters to each other and sent photos back and forth. I am sure the days were long between correspondence, and the anxiety of war and not knowing the future would crowd their thoughts. But they pressed on hoping for the day their life together would begin when he came home.

Today, our men in service have the instantaneous means of email, FaceTime, and text to keep in touch. But regardless of the method of getting news, they are still separated from family. The sacrifice of service coupled with separation reflects their total commitment to our country.

On Veterans Day, we honor all the men and women who have served our country. How do you say thank you to generations of heroes who fought for our freedoms and to those who guard us daily while we go about our routines? Words fail, but overwhelming gratitude fills my heart. Thank you so much for your service. Thank you for our freedom and for protecting us. We owe you a deep debt of gratitude today and every day. —*November 2014*

Prayer for My Mother

How thankful I am for my mother.
May she know that she is a gift to my life.
Her touch on my life will transcend generations.
And her spirit will live in all of us.

May my life be a reflection of her love
that she has shared with me all my life.
May she know that my talents and creativity
are from her and that she makes each day special.

At the end of my life, if I have been half the mother she is,
my children will have been lucky.
Her love knows no limit and is unconditionally given.
Thank you, God, for this precious gift—my Mother.

My Mother

My mother has always been the live wire in our family. She is at the helm of all mischief. No one can sit by her in church as she always finds humor in everything and will always get you tickled about something. I often joke that my dad raised three children and Mom.

Inez Norton, or "Mimi" as her grandchildren and great-grandchildren call her, always looks for the best in people. What a gift that is. She can always recognize when you need a pat on the back or a kind word of encouragement or just need to eat a piece of cake (sometimes a whole cake depending on the conversation).

My granddaughter, Amelia, seems to be following in Mimi's footsteps. She already enjoys humor in her daily conversations. She is another one you don't want to sit with in church. Isn't it amazing the things we pick up from people we admire and love?

Growing up, every day was an adventure as Mom boasted that she would never have sent us to school if Dad hadn't made her. There was just too much to do to be bothered with school. That always intrigued me as she was her high school valedictorian and believed in education.

When my boys were young, I had to make an out-of-town trip, and Mom and Dad agreed that the children should stay with them. When I called home that evening to inquire about their day at school, I was told by one of mine that they did not attend school that day. I asked to speak to Mimi, and she politely informed me that they had more important things to do that day. I laughed inside and realized that some things will never change.

Mom understands that everyday experiences are educational, too. Making mud pies, throwing water balloons, and searching for the closest hamburger place would be the childhood memories that we grew up with.

As Mother's Day approaches, I am reminded how lucky I am to have such a wonderful mother. She turns her time and attention to the things that matter in life. There is a prayer (see opposite page) I wrote for her in my book, *Bouquets of Love*. I'd love to share it with you. *—May 2015*

Every Day is Mother's Day

In my opinion, every day is Mother's Day. Once you become a mother, there is not a day that goes by that you are not constantly thinking about your children and grandchildren. This is my 37th Mother's Day, and I remember the first one like it was yesterday.

My twins, Eric and Brian, were born right before Mother's Day in 1981. I can readily say that was my favorite Mother's Day. It was overwhelming to look in the bassinet and see two little 4-pound babies, but it was my best Mother's Day because that is what I always wanted—to be a mom.

Being a mother is something for which no one can train. There are a zillion books on the market, but nothing prepares you to be a mom. My own mom, Inez Norton, set the bar high on mothering skills. She actually misbehaved as much as we did, and still does today. We had fun every day, and she was right in the middle of it. I remember so many things she did from my childhood, including mixing Kool-Aid from the little envelope package, making Popsicles using the Tupperware molds, and baking a cake every Sunday afternoon. While all this was going on, she made clothes for my sister and me and cooked supper every night.

My boys were so much fun. There was never a dull moment in our lives. While they are twins, they had very little in common growing up. Brian was pasta and decadent desserts. Eric was meat and potatoes with brownies for dessert. Balancing that was always a challenge. Dinnertime was when we shared our stories of the day. Moms are never prepared for the heartaches, discouragements, and disappointments. We do well with accomplishments and As on schoolwork, but helping a child work through tough times is a navigational feat. And no one could ever have described to me the protective instincts of a mom. At times, I knew I could defeat an army for my kids.

One of my favorite mornings was a rainy day when we decided a walk would be nice. We put on our raincoats over our summer shorts and grabbed our umbrellas. We walked around our neighborhood stomping puddles on each other! It was just a lively competition. I would love to do that today with them and add the grandkids to the fun.

When we started the *Just CrossStitch* magazine, my sons had just turned 2 years old. I had stepped away from the world of corporate accounting to work from home. I will tell you that it was a comedy machine to try to start a business while raising twin boys. I had fun watching them swing from the chandelier as I was stitching something, and we worked to get the magazine ready to print. They were so much a

part of the business because we started it in my home, and they were around all the time. I loved having them around, but NEVER in a million years did I think they would be a part of the business like they are now. I love working with them!

Each child is unique with gifts and talents that only they have. Embracing that is the key. Eric and Brian are still different, and that is a great thing. Their talents complement each other as they lead our company. I told them as they were growing up, "No one will ever love you like your mother." I believe that is the truest statement ever made. My mom's love is unconditional, and I know this every day. If my boys don't remember anything else, I pray they will always remember that I will love them unconditionally.

Mom, I love you. Thank you for being a role model and for loving us unconditionally. Eric and Brian, I am proud to be your mom. I love you. *—May 2018*

My Siblings

Today, in a marketing meeting, we were laughing about the pecking order of children in the family. I am the oldest; my brother, Keith, is the middle child and only boy, and then there's Janice, the baby.

The subject soon turned to baby books and photos, and Janice immediately chimed in that her baby book has very little in it. Mine, however, is filled out to completion. I have my first haircut samples, first baby tooth pulled, all the first birthday cake photos, and all the cards that were sent when I was born, complete with the gift list. Also included are my pediatrician visits, and each required shot was documented to perfection. I'm telling you, it's all there! I can only imagine my mom sitting there completing this journal of babyhood for me. The little book was satin with cute baby adornments on the cover.

Janice says hers has her name in it and two pages filled out. But she grinned and quickly quipped, "My parents just kept having babies until they got what they wanted!" OK, Janice won that one!

Janice is a wonderful baby sister. She survived all the mess Keith and I brought her way. We realized that because she was the youngest, she had a gift for swaying our parents in her favor. When she got married, I wrote her husband a letter explaining that because she is the baby, she is spoiled. I simply wanted him to know what to expect and how things were going to work. He just laughed.

To this day, when something goes awry, Janice, as a youngest child, always says, "It's your fault; you did it!" Once the baby, always the baby. *—January 2015*

Living with My Sister . . . Again!

In one of my last blogs, I told you the story of Neal and me packing our belongings and getting things ready for storage. But what I didn't tell you is that our house is not ready, and Neal and I moved in with my sister, Janice, and her husband, Allen.

When she offered to let us to move into their house during this interim period, we accepted and were welcomed with open arms. We moved into our place on the second floor. It wasn't long before I flashed back to our childhood. I have not lived with this person (the baby of the family) since 1978. We shared a room and had matching twin beds. She had her side of the room, and I had mine. But we had one dresser—which worked out fine except for the top drawer. This drawer posed a problem because we each had the same number of drawers except for this one. So, I took a marker pen and drew a line down the middle of it, creating borders for us both. Janice still has that dresser and reminds me of it occasionally.

On the day we delivered the final load to the storage facility, our friends and family came to rescue us by taking our personal things over to my sister's house so we could vacate promptly. That is where I lost control of my stuff. Janice had set aside a sitting room as the holding room until we could move our stuff upstairs to our new quarters. Anything that was not going to storage was going to Janice's, including Eric and Brian's kindergarten artwork and my grandchildren's notes and pictures.

The first night we were there, Neal and I decided to go to the refrigerator in the garage and grab our stash of Diet Cokes. We got to the door and realized the alarm was on. We had no idea how to get into the garage without setting it off. Since the others had already turned in for the night, we returned upstairs with water in hand. Janice told us the procedure the following day. Check!

The first week, I wore the same shoes every day as I had no idea where the others were packed. This past weekend, we decided to sift through the holding room and really find out what we brought. It was very interesting. I did find some of my shoes, but not the ones I thought I had. And I am still not sure why I brought three empty boxes.

A couple of nights ago, Neal decided he would go down and look for something he needed. So as not to disturb the early-to-bed couple, he used his flashlight. I watched with humor as he made his way down the steps and into the sitting room we were using as storage, right next to their bedroom. All I could think of was how he totally resembled a burglar! And I truly hoped he didn't wake them up or, worse, scare them. I had visions of the police being called or Neal getting attacked by the master of the home defending his castle! —*January 2017*

"Being an overprotective mother and grandmother, I could not possibly let my children's kindergarten artwork go to storage (they are 35 years old now) nor could I ever think of my grandchildren's precious notes and vibrant pictures going there either. So, I packed them up in a special box and moved them to my sister's. These treasured documents are somewhere in the sitting room in the middle of stacks of stuff . . . with me."

Phyllis

Picking Out Paint with Sister

The saga continues. Last week, I needed to select paint colors for the new house. This is like going to a candy store and trying to decide which color jelly beans to buy—they're all so tempting! I went to the paint store, bought their fan deck of paint, and took it back to my new home with Sister. I spread it out on the kitchen table and started to plan the walk (in my mind) through the house. I usually opt for more colonial, subdued colors or neutrals with pops of color in the textiles and fabrics.

As I fanned out the color charts, here she comes. "You should add some color in your life! You are so boring," she tells me. Immediately, my heart skipped a beat. She let me know that bright green was the Pantone Color of the Year, and I should incorporate this into my paint scheme. Bright green, apple green, acid green, and whatever else you want to call it . . . it is green. Now, you know I am a blue and white girl, so I sat there in total disbelief that my sister would suggest that I step outside my signature color palette.

Hearkening back to our growing up, my sister and I have always been polar opposites in most things (except the Southern rules that mom taught), especially in our choice of clothes and colors. She always opted for the ruffles and lace on a full-skirted dress. I would always choose a sailor dress or coat dress. Hers would scream pink; mine didn't. I wear solid colors, and she wears everything else, including animal prints and florals. She has always insisted that I was not "in style" and certainly not trendy. Black is my wardrobe color choice with red as the secondary color. I have a pageboy, while she sports a spiky, trendy haircut. She wears blue nail polish (or whatever the style is today), and mine is always a shade of red.

So today, she has offered the color choice of Granny Smith apple green for the ceiling in my family room. Really? I sat there and thought I should hire someone to paint her den apple green and surprise her. Just go for it, color outside the lines, and really do something daring, I thought. But, of course, I didn't.

I think in my guest room I will have something with apple green in it as a tribute to my sister. Isn't it funny how siblings from the same gene pool have opposite tastes? It has been a standing, lifelong debate about how dull I am and how trendy and stylish she is. I am good with it. *—February 2017*

Janice: My Side of the Story—A Sister's Tale

When Phyllis said she was going to be away for a few days for rest and relaxation, I jokingly said that I was going to take over the blog and tell my side of the story! So, here it goes.

When Phyllis and Neal were contemplating the offer on their old house, she was worrying about where they could live for a few short months. I offered my extra space in our house. Now, keep in mind that my husband and I have been empty nesters for 10 years. We are those happy empty nesters who have enjoyed seeing our children pursue their dreams and occasionally come home for short visits. So, when Phyllis texted me and asked if I was serious about them moving in with us, the first thing I did was call my husband. "Are you OK with them moving in?" I asked. Without pausing, he said, "Absolutely!"

We began the process of cleaning out and setting up a comfortable place for Phyllis and Neal to call home for a while. We wanted them to feel as welcomed as they could because, after all, they were the ones that were going to be out of their "comfort zone" for a while, not us!

I know in the years to come, we will have many fun stories and laughs about this time together. Many of them will probably be documented on this blog. We hope that it will always be remembered as a special time.

When people find out that my sister and her husband are living with us, I tell them immediately that I know she would do the same thing for me. Hospitality does not have to be some grand gesture—it is just sharing what you have with others.
—March 2017

At Sister's Still . . .

One more week 'til the move. I have to tell you what happened to me last week. I was the only one home in the morning, and I was getting ready to leave for the office. I came down from the upstairs (my perch) and realized that I didn't eat any breakfast. Upstairs in our sitting room, we have our coffee pot and a small toaster oven to get us through the morning time. Neal loves Pop-Tarts, and I don't care if I never see one ever again since that has been breakfast for the last three months.

Back to the story, I made my way downstairs, and there was this beautiful, perfect banana in the basket right on the counter. Exactly what I needed and wanted. I gathered up my stuff that I wag and drag and was making my way to the garage door. I reached out for my banana only to find it was a plastic banana with a Chiquita sticker on it.

What kind of a person keeps a plastic banana in the fruit basket? Really? I pondered this all the way to work. Why? And with a real paper sticker on it!

When we all returned home that evening, I asked in a very matter-of-fact tone, "What kind of a person keeps a plastic banana in their fruit basket?" They all laughed hysterically, and I realized I should have never revealed that I mistook it for a real one. Sister said it had been there for years—ever since her daughter was in high school. She didn't know why it was there, only that it was a family tradition.

Of course, you know the rest—every time we had anything to eat, that banana was on my plate. When anyone went to the store, they asked, "Need any bananas?" I will think of something to get them back, don't you worry. *—April 2017*

Janice: Empty Nesters Again

Well, I knew it was going to happen. We are empty nesters again. After four months of sharing our "nest," our upstairs birds have flown the coop! Phyllis and Neal moved out, and I have to say it's bittersweet. It has been a rather interesting experience to share a space with my sister after 40-something years of living apart.

There have been some great things that have come out of our time together. Phyllis did help me clean and organize my sewing room after four years of it being in chaos, and she got me interested in sewing again. I think that was her sole mission in moving in with me. She didn't judge me for all the beautiful yarn that I have accumulated for all the projects that I will someday crochet.

Saturday mornings became known as "bacon and biscuits" because that is what my sweet husband would fix all of us as we would sit around the table and laugh and share stories before we would all go our separate ways to start our chores. Phyllis and Neal looked forward to this day because it was the no Pop-Tart day. I will definitely miss those Saturdays.

I know that I will always be the "baby," and Phyllis will always be the "big" sister. She would remind my husband of this quite often during this time together. You see, Allen and I are celebrating our 35th wedding anniversary this week as we begin our next phase of empty nesting. When Allen and I got engaged, Phyllis wrote him a letter warning him about marrying the "spoiled" baby of the family. She told him on more than one occasion that her conscience was clear. He said he should have listened!

We wish Phyllis and Neal the best in their new home and will always look back on this time with many happy memories! —*May 2017*

A Tale of Two Banana Sandwiches

The other evening, Neal and I were sharing the story of his banana sandwich with our friends. Now on the surface, a banana sandwich is a simple thing—bread, mayo or peanut butter, and banana.

NOT at our house. First, let's talk about the sandwich itself. I am assuming a banana sandwich is a national favorite. It certainly is here in the South. We are raised on them, so making a banana sandwich is a ritual.

Neal and I had not been married long when I offered to make banana sandwiches for lunch. He is a peanut butter devotee, and I am tried-and-true mayonnaise. Proceeding to make mine, I quickly slapped the mayo on the bread, rapidly cut up my banana, and presto, sandwich done!

When I looked up, I saw a look of horror on Neal's face as he exclaimed, "I will make mine!" Very interesting, I thought. What unfolded next was a true revelation for us. I watched as this grown man carefully covered every inch of the bread with evenly applied peanut butter. Next, he literally cut the bananas into slices that were precisely the same size. (By this time, I had already eaten half of my sandwich.) He then proceeded to place each banana slice on the bread, nine slices evenly spaced and turned in the same direction. Oh my gosh, what a production. There were three little banana slices left, which he ate, as putting them on the sandwich would make it unbalanced.

If I had known he was going to engineer his sandwich, I would have driven him really crazy and cut my banana lengthwise instead of into little round slices. But I really don't think his heart could have taken it.

When Neal was finished, he turned to me and said, "This is the proper way to make a banana sandwich." Really? I actually took a photo of it, as this was a very interesting moment for me. I bet mine tasted the same. No, mine was probably better, because I just piled all my unevenly cut banana slices on the slice of bread.

He used a paper towel to hold his sandwich instead of a plate. To which, I promptly said, "We use plates." He was astonished and asked, "Now, why would I want to do that?" So, I ate my uneven banana sandwich on a Blue Calico plate, while he ate his precisely engineered work of art on a paper towel. This is the stuff fairy tales are made of! *—August 2018*

Brian's First Cake

I have always enjoyed baking, especially when I am able to bake with my family. I loved teaching my sons, Eric and Brian, how to bake when they were young. Brian especially took an interest, and before long, he wanted to try his hand at baking solo.

My friend Barbara was coming over for dinner one evening, and Brian wanted to make a cake to celebrate the occasion. I helped him select a recipe and then left him to his own devices.

When it was time for dessert that evening, Brian returned from the kitchen and emerged with his masterpiece. As he set the cake down on the table, Barbara and I exchanged knowing looks.

Something was not quite right about this cake. I knew from the recipe that the cake was supposed to be about 5 inches thick, yet Brian's cake was only about 1½ inches thick.

We cut ourselves small, cautious slices, and our first bite of the cake confirmed my suspicions. As I attempted to chew what tasted like chocolate-flavored rubber, I asked Brian how the baking went.

He exclaimed, "Do you know how hard it is to pour Coke from a 3-liter bottle into a teaspoon?" Barbara and I immediately burst into laughter when we realized his mistake. No wonder the cake was so chewy. He read the recipe's instructions for two teaspoons of "soda" as a soft drink instead of baking soda!

Since his first baking endeavor, Brian has come a long way. He is the editor-in-chief of *Bake from Scratch* magazine and loves to bake in his spare time (he calls himself a weekend baker). He has improved his skills from simple cakes to complex pastries, and I will now eat anything he bakes without hesitation. And most importantly, he has learned the difference between baking soda and soft drinks! *—August 2016*

Back-to-School Memories

Back to school—those words alone send chills down my spine. This year, my little grandson is going to 5-year-old kindergarten and will be there all day, from 8 a.m. to 3 p.m. Seriously? I can already see my sleepy boy with bed head trying to get up, get dressed, force down breakfast, and reluctantly go to school knowing that playtime is now restricted to the afternoon.

It was that way when my sons, Eric and Brian, were in school. I dreaded the start of school. Of course, we had the requisite parent-teacher meetings, room mother assignments, and school clothes requirements. I was laughing today with a friend who has a child now in middle school. Oh my, I remember those days as being the worst years with my boys. They didn't like anything, and they didn't really want to acknowledge that they had parents. You know, drop them at the street three blocks from the school, don't come visit for lunch, and don't wave or speak in front of friends. Fortunately, it all changes back in high school.

One morning during their middle school days, Eric and Brian came to the breakfast table arguing with each other and with me. This had become a pattern that I just didn't like. I like "happy" in the morning to set the tone for the day, especially when you are parting. One day, I had had it with the arguing, and I told them that since they chose to ruin my day, today I was going to ruin theirs. That went right over their heads . . . no reaction. As the unpleasantness continued and we loaded up for school, I had my plan.

As we neared the school, rather than slowing down at the usual drop-off spot three blocks away, I sped right up to the front door—much to their dismay. I told them goodbye, and as they were closing the car doors, I rolled down the windows and screamed, "Bye, babies! Mama loves you!"

As I drove off, I saw two boys running for the school entrance like Olympic sprinters. When I drove up that afternoon to pick them up, they were hiding behind the building's columns, looking to see if I had any more tricks up my sleeves. I simply smiled when they got in and asked, "Now, are we going to have any more unpleasant mornings?" No, ma'am. And for the rest of their school careers, breakfasts were fun, and we parted ways on a happy note. Drastic times call for drastic measures—or very creative mothering.

That story is true, and my now 33-year-old sons still remember it vividly. When it's time for your children to go back to school, well sometimes, you just have to use your intuition to make things work. *—August 2014*

"Back to school can be a stressful time for parents and children. You may have to do some creative parenting to keep things going smoothly."

Phyllis

Defining Moments

You can tell a lot by the eyes of those you love. There are so many moments that I recall with great vividness. The first time my grandson waved and yelled "I love you more" just melted my heart. My granddaughter thrilled me when she said, "Gigi, I want to learn to sew." There are so many others that I could write for days.

One moment in my life stands out vividly. It was one of those "defining moments." My son Eric was engaged to Katie, and it is the groom's family's privilege to host the rehearsal dinner. I saw this as my time to shine! Oh, my goodness! I was so excited. We made our plans down to the last detail.

A friend of mine does the most beautiful invitations made of silk. You open them like a French door with the printed card placed inside, and they are mailed in a silk box. To make it even better, she said we could sew a monogram on the silk before she assembled them.

When Katie and Eric were home, I unveiled the prototype, and we were all excited. Did I mention the silk matched the bridesmaid's dress? Really, how marvelous was this? So creative. My friend truly "outdid herself," as we say in the South.

A little time passed, and Eric came into the den after everyone had gone to bed but me. He looked me in the eyes and said, "Mom, Katie doesn't want the monograms on the invitation." I stared at him in total disbelief. What? How could this be? When I looked into his eyes, I realized that my reaction was going to set the tone for the rest of my life with Katie. Eric was in the awkward place of trying to please two women in his life: Mom and future wife. As I looked into his beautiful blue eyes, I said, "No monogram!"

Eric hugged me and said, "Thanks, Mom!" He knew that while my creative soul would have marveled at the monogram (as I would monogram everything if I could), it was more important that Katie know she is the woman in his life and has my unwavering love. He didn't want to hurt my feelings because he knew how much I loved monograms, and I knew that.

That's how it is sometimes, isn't it? We all really would like to have our own way regardless. But sometimes, the price is too high. Decisions that we make and reactions to situations can and will determine the future of relationships. The mother and daughter-in-law relationship has always been the brunt of jokes, and maybe, it's justified. A preacher summed it up beautifully when he was preaching on this very subject: "You have a situation where two women are in love with the same man."

Before their marriage, I asked Eric several times if he loved Katie more than me. He would roll his eyes and shake his head. "I love you in a different way, Mom." But I kept asking him this question every day right up to the wedding day. I asked him the same question the morning of his wedding, and he responded, "Yes, Mom, I do." I looked him in the eye and said, "You are ready to get married!" *—July 2016*

It's Graduation Time

It is graduation time across the country. Hearts are swelling with pride as proud parents and grandparents are doting on their graduates.

It is especially near and dear to us as we have had two college graduations this year. Our first graduation was Aaron's, who graduated from Georgia Tech in nuclear engineering. Neal and I were proud as a peacock when his son walked across that stage receiving his honors degree. What a glorious day! I can't believe he returns in the fall to complete his master's degree. It seems that we just moved him into that tiny dorm room yesterday, but it has been four years of hard work and dedication. Neal and I commented that Aaron had a grown-up look on his face that day. The young man that left us four years ago has grown into an adult. His face looked different, he carried himself differently, and his outlook on life is different. He has matured right before our eyes.

My niece, Beth, received her doctorate in systematic and philosophical theology from the Graduate Theological Union in Berkeley, California. She and her husband moved there several years ago and set on their journey to complete their education. Beth is the only granddaughter in our family. My brother and I each had two boys, and my sister had a boy and a girl. So, growing up, Beth was the princess, and rightfully so.

I was completely thrilled to see the red robe Beth wore, as that is my signature color. I tried her whole life to brainwash Beth into choosing red for her favorite color, too. I bought her first pair of red shoes and a dress with embroidered cherries to go with it. And we got a curly perm to complete the look, all while my sister was in the hospital birthing Beth's new brother many years ago. Beth and I are red girls (at least, I think so).

And to add to the wonderment, our grandson, Hays, is graduating from 5-year-old kindergarten. He is at a beautiful place in his life where his thoughts are about where we were going to eat to celebrate. (He was secretly hoping for pizza!)

In my book *Bouquets of Love*, there is one verse that I wrote that expresses my thoughts about all of them:

Walk with me as I grow.
Watch me as I explore life.
Love me unconditionally.

These three simple lines sum up every child's desires. They want us to walk steps with them as they grow up and watch them as they explore all the wonderful things life has to offer. But the main thing anyone wants is to be loved unconditionally.

Congratulations to all of you who have someone graduating this year. *—May 2014*

Family Treasures As Baby Shower Gifts

I have had the pleasure of attending baby showers for new moms and now grandmothers—yes, grandmothers. After all, we grandmothers need our nursery stash as well. This is proof there's no better excuse for a party than a baby shower.

When your gift giving calls for something unique for a new baby, give a gift that is special and sentimental—one that only a grandmother can give. Here are some of the items I have given to family members and close friends. When my Eric and Katie were expecting Hays, I presented them with one of Eric's outfits for Hays to wear home from the hospital. It has Eric's monogram on it, making it very special for his firstborn to wear. I hope Hays's firstborn son will wear it in years to come, and just maybe, I will still be here to see it.

A friend of mine, Martha, had crocheted blankets for my twins when they were born. When her son was expecting his first child, I found one of those blankets and gave it back to them with a note about the miles that were rocked with this blanket around my babies. I told the new parents that Martha had made the blanket, and I was giving it to them for more rocker mileage. They absolutely loved it.

When I announced that I was going to be a grandmother six years ago, one of our readers sent me her daughter's baby bowl. I was so touched and could hardly believe it. When I called to thank her, she told me that her daughter had passed away and she wanted this lovely bowl to be cherished. I cherish it, and in fact, I have it displayed in my nursery. I think about her every time I see it.

Look around your home and find family treasures to pass to your grandchildren. Sometimes, it's the legacy that makes a gift so special. Be sure and tell the story that goes with your gift. If you still have baby cups and silver spoons from your children, get them out and use them for your grandchildren and tell stories about their parents. It gives great joy to share your own stories. *—August 2014*

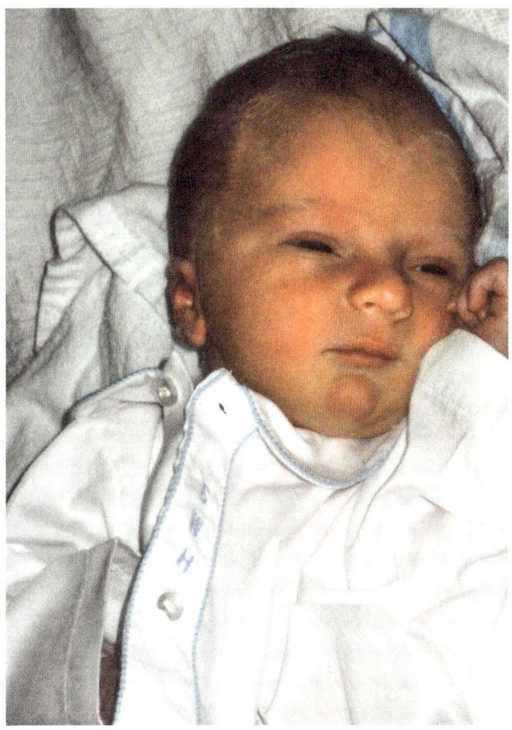

"It is amazing how strong our childhood memories are, isn't it? A song, a scent, a food will all signal a special memory."

Phyllis

Spring Break with the Grands!

We have just finished one of the most glorious weeks with our grandchildren. It was their spring break, and we got them all to ourselves! Life through the eyes of a child is so pure and right on target. They say the most amazing things and ask the most daunting questions.

We decided a wonderful day trip to Franklin, Tennessee, would be fun as my granddaughter, Amelia, and I had plotted for a visit to the American Girl doll store there. I had purchased the Felicity doll years ago, along with the tea table and canopy bed, right after my granddaughter was born in hopes that she would share my love of Williamsburg. We got the doll out and had a marvelous afternoon reading about her while sharing afternoon tea. I was in heaven! But Amelia wanted to see the newest American Girl dolls, and I thought that would be so much fun.

The guys dropped us off, and we entered the utopia of girl stores. I could not take it all in as there were so many lovely displays. How could you choose a doll? Luckily, Amelia knew the one she wanted—Julie Albright. Julie is the doll representing the 1970s, complete with a crocheted vest, bell bottoms, and flower decorations. Is she supposed to be a hippie? Who knows, but she was cute.

My grandson, Hays, on the other hand, is more of the venturesome type, and he selected an indoor trampoline experience that both of them loved. But the real adventure came when they turned on the mechanical bull. Oh, my goodness! How could my babies be riding that contraption? I realized they had grown up and were fearless. They both kept begging for the attendant to make the bull go faster and rougher until they were being thrown off (thankfully onto a heavily padded floor).

As we headed back to Birmingham, I must admit that I don't care if I see another chicken wing again. We ate those things four times, at least, and had pizza and all the things they love. It was their week, and Neal told them they could select the meals. We all got in the kitchen and cooked one day, enjoyed a fun meal around the table that night, and followed it up by watching the third and latest movie in the series *Beverly Hills Chihuahua*.

Taking them home was very sad for me. Our week was over, and I miss them so much when we are apart. This morning, Neal and I ate the last of the Lucky Charms, complete with the new Magic Unicorn marshmallows. You know, those marshmallows are just not as good when you don't have any kids with whom to enjoy them! *—April 2018*

Jump for Joy

I recently received a very special surprise. My granddaughter, Amelia, came to visit, and I had planned our activities, but she had other ideas. She announced that she was going to make a quilt for her new doll. I could have jumped for joy. Then, she said the magic words to a sewing grandmother: "Gigi, I want a sewing machine so I can make dresses for my dolls." Our sewing journey had begun.

Her sewing machine is small, and she loves it—Sofia 2 by Baby Lock. When she isn't sewing, it is perfect for me to take when I am traveling. Everyone in my office thinks it's hilarious that I travel with a sewing machine, but when Neal is attending a conference and I tag along, I love to spend part of my day sewing. OK, back on track.

I learned to sew, cook, garden, and do most things from my mom or one of my grandmothers. It occurred to me that nothing has really changed. With all of our technology, there is nothing that replaces a caring, loving person teaching something to another.

When my boys were young, they loved to cook with me, which mainly meant licking the icing off the mixer beaters. But they were in the kitchen learning, and today, they are both marvelous cooks. Brian bakes, and Eric likes to grill. They have taken the basics and have continued to learn and try new techniques and recipes.

As the grandchildren came along, I love including them in the kitchen. We have created some wonderful memories mixing and baking together. When my grandson, Hays, was very young, he loved to make biscuits. Today, cookie dough is his passion. I realized that he is just like his dad, Eric. He really is learning to cook, but he is also there to eat the icing. Amelia likes to add every ingredient, stir every stroke, and try to get the batter in the pan all on her own. She is so determined, and I love that about her.

Are we teaching as we should? As we get older and we feel that our time has passed for teaching, we forget that our knowledge should be passed along. It's the tips and tidbits of knowledge that make things interesting. We should be creating opportunities to teach. I'm sure many of you are thinking, "I don't have anyone to teach!" Let me share a story.

When I was a teenager, we went on a choir tour, which meant we stayed in homes of church members in the cities where we traveled. It was my great fortune to stay in the home of a very elderly woman who was a quilter. She had one pattern that she made that I was intrigued with—Cathedral Window. I admired her work and couldn't keep from asking a zillion questions about how she made that quilt. She went to her little box of fabric, brought out fabric, and proceeded to cut squares. She showed me how she made the quilt, sent me home with that sample, and encouraged me to get started in making a quilt.

I still have that sample block. I keep it with my quilting materials and think of her every time I look at it. You never know who in your circle of influence would love to learn from you. Whether your passion is sewing, gardening, cooking, or collecting, take time to share your interests with someone. Young people are looking for someone to teach them. *—November 2014*

Special Heirloom

I hope your 2020 has started off with great joy and happiness. We have all made our New Year's resolutions I am sure, but mine have changed over the years. Oh, yes—I have started 45 diets and resolved to get organized in my sewing room, but now, my resolutions have a different outlook.

During the Christmas season, my son Brian, who is the founding editor of our *Bake from Scratch* magazine, always bakes cookies. This year, he recreated my dad's Fruitcake Cookie recipe and brought them to all of us to enjoy. It was very interesting that he had them in a cookie tin my mom had used for years. It is a cute tin resembling a merry-go-round. Mom and Dad had received this filled with a fruitcake inside and kept the tin.

When I asked about it, Brian told me that Mom had given it to him. Brian always knew at Christmas when the cookie tin came out it meant goodies inside. Mom said she was not baking anymore, and he could have it. He has loved that tin since he was a child, and he now treasures not only the container but the magical memories he had as a young boy.

I thought about this a lot as a new year has started. One of my resolutions is to make every day as special as I can. When the grandchildren come, I want to have special dishes or containers that they will associate with fun times as they grow older. It doesn't have to be an expensive item but one they will remember as something Gigi used when they were at my house. I want it to represent a glorious time of laughter and fun around the table.

I don't believe in saving anything for a special occasion, as every day we live is special, and our friends and family are the most special. This year, I am going to focus on the little things that make each day unique, and I want my grandchildren to have wonderful memories. *—January 2020*

GLAZED FRUITCAKE COOKIES

Makes about 36 cookies

- 1¼ cups spiced rum
- ½ cup finely chopped candied red cherries
- ½ cup finely chopped candied green cherries
- ½ cup finely chopped dried pineapple
- ½ cup finely chopped crystallized ginger
- ½ cup finely chopped candied orange
- 1 cup unsalted butter, softened
- 1¾ cups granulated sugar, divided
- ¼ cup firmly packed light brown sugar
- 2 large eggs, room temperature
- 1 teaspoon rum extract
- 3½ cups all-purpose flour
- 1 teaspoon baking soda
- 1 teaspoon kosher salt
- 1 teaspoon ground nutmeg
- 1 teaspoon ground cinnamon
- 1 teaspoon ground ginger
- ½ teaspoon ground cloves
- 1 cup chopped toasted pecans
- Rum Drizzle (recipe follows)

1. In a medium microwave-safe bowl, combine spiced rum, cherries, pineapple, crystallized ginger, and orange, and heat on high until hot, 2 to 3 minutes; let stand at room temperature for at least 1 hour, stirring occasionally. Drain fruit mixture. Set aside.

2. Preheat oven to 350°. Line 4 baking sheets with parchment paper.

3. In the bowl of a stand mixer fitted with the paddle attachment, beat butter, 1¼ cups granulated sugar, and brown sugar at medium speed until fluffy, 2 to 3 minutes, stopping to scrape sides of bowl. Add eggs, one at a time, beating well after each addition. Beat in rum extract.

4. In a medium bowl, whisk together flour, baking soda, salt, nutmeg, cinnamon, ground ginger, and cloves. Add flour mixture to butter mixture all at once; beat at low speed just until combined, stopping to scrape sides of bowl. Fold in fruit mixture and pecans. (Dough will be sticky.)

5. Place remaining ½ cup granulated sugar on a rimmed plate. Using a 2-tablespoon spring-loaded scoop, scoop dough, and shape into balls. Roll in sugar, and place 1½ to 2 inches apart on prepared pans. Using the palm of your hand, gently flatten balls to 1-inch thickness.

6. Bake until light golden brown and set around the edges, about 12 minutes. Let cool on pans for 3 minutes. Remove from pans, and let cool completely on wire racks. Place Rum Drizzle in a piping bag, and cut a ¼-inch opening in tip. Drizzle onto cooled cookies.

RUM DRIZZLE

Makes about ½ cup

- 1 cup confectioners' sugar
- 1½ tablespoons heavy whipping cream
- 1 tablespoon spiced rum
- 2 teaspoons unsalted butter, melted
- ¼ teaspoon kosher salt

1. In a medium bowl, whisk together all ingredients, mixing well until smooth. Use immediately.

Grandchildren Traditions

When I was growing up, there were things that you could count on when you were visiting grandparents. My mom's dad always took us fishing! With cane poles hanging out the windows, we got in his white Chevrolet Bel Air, and off we would go.

I was not a fan of worms, so Granddad Hill showed us how to make bread balls, and the fish loved them. We would attach red-and-white bobbing corks to the line, so we could see when we got a bite and would attempt to snag the fish. We would bring our catch home, and then Mom would cook them. Later, she confessed she bought fish sticks and passed them off as our catch, but we were so young we didn't know the difference. What we do remember is the outing with all our cousins to the lake to fish.

When we got cleaned up and had dinner, Granddad always had an old-fashioned ice cream churn on hand with the homemade vanilla ice cream mixture ready to freeze. After dinner, we took turns cranking the handle until the ice cream was frozen. We thought that was so much fun!

These are precious memories from trips to visit the grandparents. My grands today always expect certain things at our home. For instance, we tape old *Gunsmoke* movies for our grandson, and we have a movie marathon until late in the evening. Pajamas, movies, and popcorn—it's something they look forward to. It's just tradition! *—March 2019*

The Joy of Little Girls

When our granddaughter, Amelia, was born, my life took on a whole new meaning. My babies were twin boys, and my first grandchild was a boy. Now, don't get me wrong; I love my boys more than life. I have laughed often and said that I am a great boy mom.

But when Amelia was born three years ago, I finally got my girl. I had squirreled away antique lace, linen, buttons, ribbons, and vintage garment patterns since I was expecting my boys 33 years ago. I would visit my stash from time to time and wonder if I would ever get to use my collection. As soon as I learned my daughter-in-law was expecting a girl, I started sewing for her, monogramming everything, and searching for the perfect shoes.

I have just lived through the most amazing thing in the world: Amelia's first dance recital. She is 3 going on 20 and loves bows, ribbons, and dresses that "twirl," so she was in her element. As we entered the theatre and saw that enormous stage, I really wasn't sure she would even go out there. It is overwhelming enough for adults to be before hundreds of people, but babies?

There were hundreds of doting families waiting to see their little angels perform, all with flowers in hand for the presentation and photos afterwards. Hollywood could not do better. I picked roses from my garden and made my small presentation nosegay.

Finally, after several other groups had performed, out they came from behind the curtain. Little arms and legs were flailing in all directions with reckless abandon. And each had a time for their run-and-jump ballerina solo. Amelia's was perfect.

The scene was quite comical. I loved watching the girls stop and wave to their families. One couldn't get her hair bow back on her head. Two started pushing each other trying to stand on the same star. I was having so much fun watching these 3-year-olds on stage. Wouldn't it be fantastic to really know what thoughts they have as they are going through their dance?

I love Jackie Kennedy's words: "The children have been a wonderful gift to me, and I'm thankful to have once again seen our world through their eyes." *—May 2014*

Camp Gigi: Part 1

Camp Gigi has just finished. It was a full week of having my granddaughter, Amelia, at our home with her best friend joining us for part of the week. Her brother, Hays, was at his camp in the mountains, so it worked out perfectly for Amelia to come to stay with us. Camp Gigi is a week free of electronic devices, where creativity is the objective.

Our time together began with coloring quilt blocks for our Mrs. Noah Quilt. Each block features animals and the characters from the biblical story of Noah's ark, including a really fun boat. This quilt was originally intended to be appliquéd, but for an 8-year-old girl, that was way too complicated, so we opted for fabric pens and colored the blocks in cute patterns.

A great awakening for me was making slime. Now, let me stop here and tell you that the makers of glue have masterminded a genius concept for kids making slime. I have never bought school glue by the gallon before, but now, I can check that one off my list. Believe it or not, we used almost the entire gallon. This modern replacement of modeling clay is made up of shaving cream, glue, glitter, baking soda, and contact lens solution. Wow, that alone was a weird thing to see. We manufactured bowls of this stuff and then filled plastic storage bags with our daily creation. I kept asking, "What do you do with this stuff?" Only to get the same answer over and over: "You play with it." Well, OK, we'll play with it, then.

One of my favorite things we did during the week was make our notebooks. We took spiral-bound notebooks and ribbon remnants and tied a ribbon into every ring. The girls had so much fun making these wild displays of color! I am unsure if the notebooks will pass school regulations, but they are fun to have and enjoy.

What else did I learn from the girls? They are smarter than me. They taught me how to use my cell phone in ways I never knew possible. I am now accomplished in making weird videos on my phone, if anyone needs a tutorial.

Despite the various devices we have at our fingertips, kids still love to create with their hands. All they really want is your time and attention. I will share the rest of my grandmother journey with you later. *—July 2018*

PS: Neal said he will have Camp Neal for our grandson whenever he can schedule him, and it won't include making slime.

Camp Gigi: Part 2

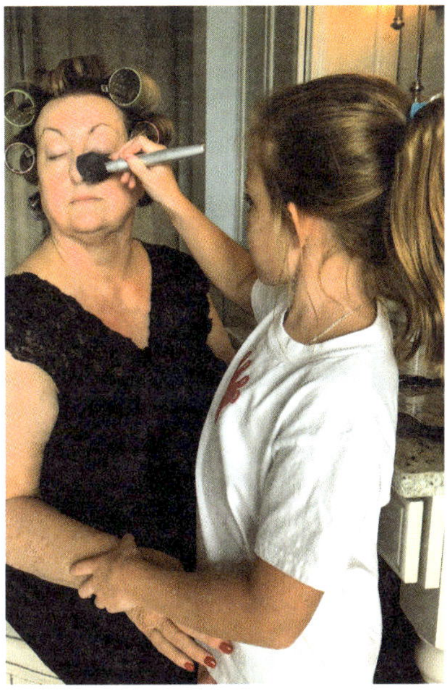

One of the main things I wanted to do with the girls at Camp Gigi is to get them working with the mind and hands—creativity is key. One thing I've noticed is that we all need more creative time, and it's even more fun if we work with others. My granddaughter and her best friend encouraged each other, and their creativity was flowing freely.

Interestingly, they started out trying to make things alike, and then we talked about being an individual. I assured them there was no right or wrong way to create their totes or T-shirts. These projects were distinctly theirs, and that was what made them special.

However, I did purchase some matching iron-ons. I have learned that if you don't provide some alike items, someone will inevitably feel slighted. So, the composition of their designs is what would make them unique. I loved listening to their giggles and side conversations as they moved their motifs around a million times.

The entire day's event culminated with a wonderful fashion show—and I loved every moment of it! The next day was the most interesting day I have had in a long time. The two bright-eyed wonders had planned that this would be the day they would do my hair and makeup. They were giddy, and I was a little . . . hesitant? As they proceeded to arrange my powders, shadows, and mascara, I realized these girls know more at 8 years old than I knew at 15.

One of them asked where the moisturizer was, because apparently, I was in desperate need. From then on, the makeover was in full swing. They made me promise I would wear it all day. OK, I can do this, I told myself. Besides, was "no" ever really an option? *—July 2018*

Mom enjoyed time spent visiting with family and made an annual trip to New Orleans in October to have birthday tea with Katie and Amelia. She believed that the time we spend together would become memories that would be cherished forever.

—Brian and Eric

Creating Special Moments

First, let me thank you for all your lovely emails of encouragement regarding my anemia. You all are the loveliest people. What a blessing in my life!

This past weekend, my granddaughter, daughter-in-law, and I went to our annual tea celebrating our birthdays. To my surprise, it was a Halloween-themed tea, and the tearoom buzzed with great excitement. The Windsor Court in New Orleans has a superb tearoom and is steeped in tradition, but on this day, it was all about fun. It is amazing that they can maintain elegance and still have a themed party like this. Everyone was thrilled to see the movie character Maleficent singing and visiting the tables. All fun for all ages.

Memories. We were all creating memories. I think these past two years of being separated because of the pandemic have made us all cherish the time we have with family and friends. Perhaps, we took for granted that we would always have freedom to go anywhere and visit. But the COVID-19 virus changed all that. We relied on memories to get us through times of loneliness and vowed to create as many new ones as soon as we could.

I cherish time with family and friends so much more. Every moment is important and should be treated that way. As we have opportunities, let's step out and do something fun. Call more often and always take photos when you can. Time is a precious gift. —*October 2021*

Œuvres Complètes pour
J. S. Bach
Love Lifted Me
545
Love Is the Theme

On Faith & Encouragement

SHARING THE GIFT OF MUSIC

ONE OF THE JOYS OF MY LIFE was knowing and playing alongside our darling Phyllis. She and I were the organ/piano duo in our church for 15-plus years. We enjoyed the "give and take" of playing together that comes around once in a lifetime. She was such a blessing to me! Phyllis taught me lots of things, and my family and I adored her.

If you had the privilege of spending time with her, you most likely laughed until your sides ached. She was not only hilarious but also brilliant, wise, and very generous.

Phyllis loved sharing her faith, her resources, and her gift of music with others. What a blessing she was to so many! Her offering to our Lord was her ministry through music. She loved worshipping Him and helping to equip fellow believers through her playing. And she did that so well! Even as her publishing empire flourished, she never missed playing the organ at church on Sundays. She knew from whom her varied and plentiful abilities came, and she played His praises without fail.

Phyllis was a genius who was way ahead of her time—a trailblazer in women-owned businesses. She had a vision and the skills necessary to accomplish that vision. Though she "rubbed elbows" with many celebrities, she never failed to acknowledge and encourage her associates and colleagues. She treated employees as friends and helped them whenever specific needs arose. Phyllis was an inspiring servant of our Lord.

She left behind a legacy of love and service. What a joy to have worked with and received inspiration from her! I will treasure her memory always. —*Cheryl Ramsey, friend and pianist*

Cheryl Ramsey

An Encouraging Word

It's a new year, and I am already late on my first post for 2023. January was a blur. But February is here, and we are enjoying these beautiful days. It's still cold, but the light is brighter.

Our Ribbon group is very special to me. I love your notes and emails. You are so encouraging. Together, we can bring light into our lives by sharing thoughts and experiences.

What makes us respond to an encouraging word? Have you ever thought about it? My mom passed away last year, and I miss her so much. She had the special gift of noticing and commenting on the good in people. She always found something genuine to talk about that made you feel special. It just took a tiny sentence, and your day was changed.

As we begin this new year together, let's take a baby step forward in encouraging people in our lives. It must be genuine, not contrived. Pointing out good brings a new belief in oneself. It's also a very good habit to adopt. It will become a part of your life as you encounter people.

Our world today needs to see love and concern in people. We can lift the cloud with carefully chosen words. Today, go out and be a shining light of encouragement. You will change a life. —*February 2023*

What Is My Worth?

I have watched the most amazing TV commercials lately where women are encouraged to be ahead of everyone—leader of the pack, room mother extraordinaire, best laundress in town—at any cost. I just chuckle when I see this as it perfectly describes being a woman. We women have always been able to do all that and more, but it doesn't describe our worth. Those are things that we do—and not who we are.

But the question is often posed: What are we worth? It's a tough question. We are worth so much, it can't be described to anyone. Our worth to our friends, family, and colleagues is different for each. I have friends who are worth so much; just hearing their voices makes my day special. My precious family is worth everything to me.

We are constantly challenged as to our worth as a woman, and when the question is posed, my answer is: everything. It's not about accomplishments or wealth; it's about loving unconditionally, encouraging others, reaching out a hand to those in need, praying for and with friends who are hurting, and being an example of living our lives in such a way that our family and friends know we are always there for them.

If you are letting your accomplishments define your worth, please look into your heart to find your worth there instead. Right now, call someone and make their day. You will see your worth come to life. You are worth everything. *—February 2023*

Looking Ahead

As we are ending 2022, I thank you all for your lovely emails, texts, and cards. It was a hard year for our family, as Mom passed away this summer, and many of you know all that entails. I still struggle with this rare anemia, and you have offered up meaningful prayers for me, and I thank you. Still fighting and praying.

I have not written to you in quite a while, and many of you have reached out. Thank you. I have learned more about perseverance during this time than I could have imagined. But we must all go forth and never give up. Never lose hope. I think you must live it to really understand it.

This time of year is hard for so many, and finding joy is difficult. Just when you think you have it nailed—boom—something else seems to pop up. I have started looking at these moments as another trail on my journey. We all must stop and evaluate how blessed we are in so many ways, and these challenges will make us stronger.

Next year, we will start *Ribbon in My Journal* with a fresh outlook of encouragement and finding joy. Our family wishes you a blessed Christmas and holiday season. I am thankful for you and for being a part of Ribbon. Thank you for your love and concern! We will go forth together. *—December 2022*

Neal
Phyllis
Brian
Morgan
Aaron
Eric
Katie
Hays

Creating Joy

Christmas 2021 is here, and all the children are running on adrenaline. I remember that feeling well. School is almost out for the holiday break, and kids are counting the days. Coming from a year of being confined during the pandemic, all of us feel life is beginning again, even though we still have to contend with the COVID-19 virus.

I think we live differently now than we did before. I have learned that being quiet and staying inside can be very nice. Being content with ourselves and what we are surrounded with is peaceful. A dear friend said to me that she loved her life as it was before the pandemic and misses it terribly. I think we all feel that way, too. One thing is for sure: Each day is unpredictable, isn't it?

My greatest joy is seeing the holiday sparkle in children's eyes. I love the choir programs at church, where they are singing their little hearts out dressed in special outfits. I wish we could capture that innocence for a long time. It's so important to let children be children. The giggles and laughter and smiles and hugs are all a part of being a child. And don't forget to put a dot of cookie icing on their little noses. It creates a moment of cheerfulness that will not be forgotten.

We have a wonderful man at our church known as the candy man. He always hands me a peppermint for a smile. He only rewards smiles. I think he is very special and brings a moment of happiness whenever I see him.

I hope our lives are such that when people encounter us, they have a moment of joy. I can only imagine the moment at the manger when the shepherds saw the Christ child. What a wondrous night when the quiet, calm darkness was interrupted with the greatest gift ever! Merry Christmas to you, and may you create cheerful moments for those around you. *—December 2021*

Turning the Page

There comes a day when you realize turning the page is the best feeling in the world, because you realize there is so much more to the book than the page you were stuck on."
—Zayn Malik, British singer and songwriter

I read this most interesting statement the other day written by British singer Zayn Malik. It really struck a nerve with me. I flashed back to high school chemistry when I would read and reread the same page over and over. I realized that I glazed over halfway down, and my eyes would scan the page without any comprehension of what I was reading. Then, I would go back to the top and reread the same page, glazing over at the same place. Finally, I would want to give up. Unfortunately, in school, we had to understand each page before we could go on.

In life, I find that mentally and emotionally we become stuck on a current situation or event that has occurred in our lives. It may be a tragedy, an illness, or a difficult situation we are dealing with, and we just can't seem to move past it. We replay it over and over in our minds and find we are still at the same place.

It is hard to let go and move on, isn't it? But when we do, it is refreshing. How do we move on past our circumstances? How do we get something out of our minds that seems to haunt us?

First, decide if there is anything you can do to change it. If we can't change a situation, then why are we letting it occupy our thoughts? We have to fill our minds with other thoughts and not let it take over.

Second, if there is something you can do to right a situation, then do it. That's the hard one. It may be going to a person and apologizing or clearing up a misunderstanding. Most of the time, we have made the situation bigger than it really is.

Finally, if there has been a tragedy or loss in your life, moving past it is hard. Turning the page to a new life seems impossible, but the best option may be to find a dear friend in whom you can confide. Sharing our thoughts, fears, and hurts with someone will lighten our loads. You can't rush time, and turning the page may take a while, but be aware that turning the page is moving forward with anticipation.

As I write my thoughts today, I can recall many times in my life where I just had to turn the page to a new beginning. Turn the page today and open your heart to new days ahead. *—August 2015*

"Renew your focus and appreciate the beautiful things that add joy to busy days."

Phyllis

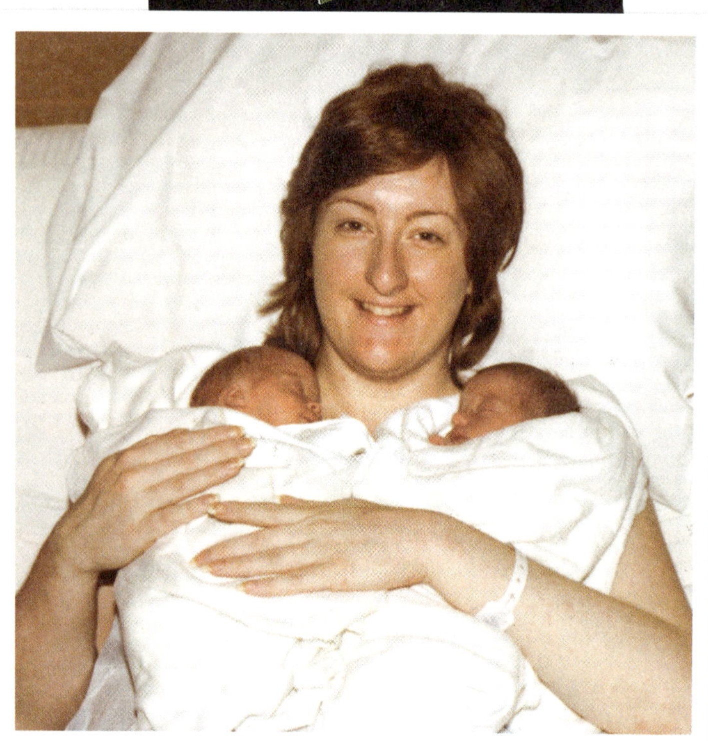

New Beginnings

I have been pondering the phrase "new beginnings" as it pertains to this new year. I am trying to find something new, as it appears this year is shaping up to look a lot like 2020. Masks, social distancing, pandemic protocols—you know the drill. But it is a new year.

The beginning of a new year excites me. When I was a child, for some strange reason, I felt the need to tidy up my room that I shared with my sister, Janice. We would get in there and really shape it up. It was restorative to move things around and discard things that we thought we would keep forever. I think back on those days with great fondness.

What do we keep and what do we discard? I want to keep a spirit of gratefulness for the things in my life that I love. Keeping a grateful heart is reminding ourselves constantly of the good in our lives. I don't know about you, but I can be pulled down quickly in my thoughts. It's at that time I must remind myself of blessings. It's little things like my snowdrops coming up in the flower bed and notes from friends. Family, friends, and wonderful people that I work with give great meaning to my life. Time with my grandchildren is the best treasure.

I want to keep a creative spirit. I love to sew and quilt, along with playing the piano. I have lost that creative spirit during this pandemic. Today, I am going to begin a creative journey of finishing some sewing projects that I started, dragging out tote bags of needlework and enjoying every stitch—even if I only have time to make a few stitches.

Discarding is easy for me. I am discarding TV shows that do not refresh, restore, or give me encouragement. I am a hopeless romantic and can still watch *The Sound of Music* a million times and rejoice when the magnificent organ sounds for the wedding march. I love *White Christmas*, especially the "Sisters" song, and I marvel at the tiny waists and stunning garments that are worn. Who doesn't love old movies? I watched *Pillow Talk* with Doris Day and immediately set about to find vintage patterns for those fabulous coats she wore. When I finish watching something, I want to have a song in my heart and feel good. Is that total reality? No, but I don't need or want any more reality.

Discouragement has occupied all our thoughts during this time. Let's discard that and find ways to replace it with hope, faith, and love. Let's have hope that this pandemic will be over soon, faith that our doctors will continue to develop cures, and love for those who have been touched by this or who have fears. —*January 2021*

Faith, Hope, and Love

My grandmother gave me a silver charm for my charm bracelet when I was a little girl. I still have it on my bracelet today. "Faith, Hope, and Charity." I don't think I really understood the words on it then or why she loved that charm so much. It came from a little store in her town called The Jewel Box. It was a big deal to me to get a gift from that store. I understand it now. My silver charm is a prized possession of mine. But more important are the words and meaning that are prized today in this time of great uncertainty.

Faith and hope go hand in hand. We must always have faith in God. When I feel panicky, I have to be still and think about that. Hope keeps me going, too. "Charity" in Christian writings is the highest form of love, indicating the reciprocal love between God and humans, which is demonstrated when we show unselfish love to one another.

The phrase is based on the Bible verse 1 Corinthians 13:13 (NIV): "And now these three remain: faith, hope and love. But the greatest of these is love." (The King James Version uses "charity" instead of "love.")

The greatest is love. Love today is being demonstrated in so many ways. During this COVID-19 virus outbreak, our health professionals are working endlessly to minister to patients, neighbors are helping the elderly, schools and organizations are feeding children, and people are connecting at a new level.

Our sewing ladies are making masks for medical personnel who simply have none. These are gifts of love and concern to those they don't even know. That is so wonderful. I have seen children gathering food for food banks and schools. That brings tears to my eyes. At a very early age, they are learning about love and doing what they can do to help. I could write for hours about what I have seen that I call "love in action."

Working together blurs all lines of race, nationality, political party, and age. How refreshing! It's neighbor helping neighbor to survive and come out on the other side of this pandemic a better nation. I pray that we will always love each other as we have during these days.

Faith will be our foundation and rock.

Hope will lead us on this journey of unknown days.

And love will be the greatest gift we can give and receive.

May God give you peace and comfort during these days. We are all one in this, and together we will go forward. —*March 2020*

Thoughts from My Heart

I find my thoughts drifting these days to a state of disbelief as I watch the news. In fact, I can hardly watch the news anymore. I want to say, "Stop the madness! Everyone, breathe!" The best way for me to navigate these uncertain times is to focus on helping people around me. It is my hope that we can change lives and hearts one at a time.

My thoughts this weekend turned to my beloved Big Oak Ranch where children of many different backgrounds live together as one. These precious little ones were placed at the ranch because they have no parents or the ones that they do have discarded them. Most of these children were abused or neglected. They come with fear in their hearts, longing for someone to love them.

I became involved with Big Oak Ranch over 10 years ago. I was asked to visit the ranch and school by friends of mine. I really didn't know how I was going to react to this place, as my usual response is to shut down. The thought of any child hurting or being hurt makes me crazy.

I met this beautiful young woman named Rachel Fisher. She had been at the ranch for several years, along with her sister Trinity. These two beautiful young women just made the room happier when they entered. Rachel captured my heart from the moment I met her. Rachel, who was very witty and very inquisitive, walked up to me and asked, "Who are you?" I introduced myself and told her I was visiting the ranch as I had never been there before. I just adored her feistiness as we talked for a few minutes.

She had beautiful green eyes and a smile that would melt butter. Her smile was mischievous, and she was a pistol. I knew I had just met someone who really intrigued me, and I loved her instantly.

It was that day I knew God was calling me to be involved with Big Oak Ranch. John Croyle, the founder of Big Oak, asked me if I was involved or committed. Wow, that was a question I had not anticipated. I responded, "Committed!" It was because of Rachel that I felt that the ranch needed a Ladies Auxiliary to support the work there.

In 2006, Phyllis and Alabama philanthropist Joann Bashinsky formed the Big Oak Auxiliary as a fundraising and volunteer service group to promote Big Oak Ranch's goal of giving abused, neglected, and abandoned children a solid Christian home and chance to fulfill God's plan for their lives. As part of her dedication to the project, Phyllis and Hoffman Media would sponsor the children at Big Oak in a shopping day at Target just before Christmas. Each employee would help a child spend $100. The event was done in memory of Hoffman's own employee Micki Reis, who died saving her child from drowning in 2005. —*Brian and Eric*

The girls' and boys' ranches were kept separate, very wisely, and at each place, the children were divided into homes. Each home has a set of house parents whose life is committed to raising this wonderful group of children. They have so much sadness and abuse to work through. There were things that I thought an auxiliary could do to help these wonderful parents by supplementing the operating budgets they have.

There were 10 of us who met to start the Ladies Auxiliary. We all knew we could be instrumental in this ministry. Our numbers and the work of the auxiliary has grown to include gifts, clothing, etc., for these children and to be a support group for the house mothers.

Back to Rachel—I was there when she graduated from high school. I watched her walk across the stage and get her diploma with aspirations of being an aesthetician. I wanted to help her, and in fact, I had proposed the idea of her coming to live with me in the fall so I could help her get started. We had our plans, and I was so excited that I was going to be a part of her life. I know she had blessed mine, and I was hoping I could do the same for her.

It was only a few weeks later that John Croyle called to tell me that Rachel had been killed in an automobile accident. My heart was broken, and it still is today. It's not mine to understand why this happened, as I know God is in control. I felt a huge loss that day. As time has passed, I can still see her beautiful face and witty smile. It has been 10 years ago this week.

Events like this change us in so many ways. Our work has gone on, and there are over 2,000 children who have come through Big Oak Ranch and go on to become responsible adults. It is important to break the cycle of abuse and neglect and go out into the world, establishing homes where children are loved. Rachel's sister Trinity works at the ranch now, and it brings great joy to me to watch her change lives.

Paula Deen came for our first fundraiser to get us going. And that was the shot in the arm we needed. Joe Namath joined in along with Bart Starr, Taylor Hicks, and Jeannie Robertson for fundraisers in the next few years. In September, Amy Grant is coming for our 2016 fundraiser. What a marvelous woman to give of her time to our auxiliary.

I don't have any answers or any opinions about life other than knowing that I want to make a difference. There are probably organizations in your area where you can make a difference. When someone knows another cares for them and loves them, it changes hearts and lives. Let's make a difference every day! *—July 2016*

Seeing Beauty

"The sign of a beautiful person is that they always see beauty in others."
—Omar Suleiman, American Islamic Scholar and civil rights activist

I thought about this quote, as I have read it many times, and it resonates with me now more than ever. We are drawn to those who find beauty in all things because such a practice is not always common. And I call it a practice because it is sometimes unnatural to see the good and proclaim it to those around us.

It's a choice. We must focus on the positive things around us. For it is what we look at that feeds our thoughts, and it is our thoughts that feed the heart. Choosing to look at the small things that bring joy makes such a difference.

A beautiful flower blooming, hugs from my precious grandchildren, and coffee with Neal while watching the sun come up—these are tiny moments that I cherish.

The problems that we have will be what they are. So, as we work through them, let's remember the lovely moments in our lives and let that overflow into the way we speak and act.

In a world where people are constantly finding fault in everyone and everything, I am encouraged by those who breathe fresh air into a room with their words. Let us all strive to be that person today and every day. *—July 2018*

You Are Valuable

I am moved by the events of last week—the tragic suicide deaths of well-known people who appeared to have everything! It proves that suffering does not discriminate based on income level. Kate Spade was a lady I admired for years. As she began her business and expanded it, she set fashion trends for women around the world. Her look was simple and fresh and delighted so many. How do you write about something like this? I wish I had all the answers, but no one does.

I don't know what Kate's specific situation was and don't want to speculate. But the media coverage surrounding her suicide made me pause to think and made me want to share an important reminder: you—all of us—are valuable.

The feelings and concerns that remain after someone takes their life are something I am familiar with, as years ago I experienced the results of the suicide death of a member of our church. What did I miss? How could I have helped?

I offer these thoughts today for all of us to think about. There are times in our lives when we are vulnerable to developing depression. Change is hard, and sometimes, an event can trigger feelings of worthlessness. As women, we often want to feel needed, and when we think that we are not, then feelings of depression can creep in. It is real; it is hard, and it hurts. Sometimes, depression can develop without an obvious trigger.

In spite of what you may be feeling during one of these times, please remember this: you are valuable, and you are beautiful. Whenever you experience the feeling that you are not, please say something. Reach out. Don't be afraid to seek professional help. Trust me, no one will ever think less of you.

Many times, it is the person we think is the strongest who might be suffering the most. Strong people feel they have to be the rock for everyone else and cover up their own feelings. Pay close attention to this. Draw close to all your friends and have heart-to-heart talks. It is refreshing and renewing to share your inner thoughts with someone who loves you. That may be all it takes—to know someone cares and can offer support and love.

Now, go out there and sparkle! Be the best friend you can be to others God placed in your life. You are valuable, and you are treasured. You make the world a better place. I have no idea who wrote this, but I jotted it down, and it means so much to me: "God often uses our deepest pain as the launching pad of our greatest calling."
Reach out, always. *—June 2018*

Reignite

I was in my doctor's office this week, and a new nurse practitioner came in. I greeted her and asked about her new career. She made the most wonderful statement: "Being here has reignited me—I love this!" My doctor looked at me and said, "That is a great word."

Reignite—meaning to ignite again. I thought about that on the way home and pondered many things. As we see on the news often, forest fires will reignite after firefighters think they are out. There is a small ember somewhere underneath the rubble that keeps burning and eventually reignites into a full-blown fire.

Our souls are a lot like that. For various reasons, our zeal for things in our life is dampened and many times extinguished. What causes this? I think it's discouragement, disappointment, failed attempts, hurt, or just the mundane ritual of something that gets very old. When we have been disappointed by something, it can take away our spirit. We are wounded, hurt, and sometimes damaged.

I have experienced that very thing this week. I have shared with you my love of gardening. We planted 50 roses in the spring, and I have lived in hopes of looking out and seeing this complete garden covered in blooms. This past week, we were trimming this horrible red leaf thing off some of them and realized something was wrong. Upon doing a little research, I discovered a disgusting rose disease called witches' broom had completely infiltrated our garden. There is no cure, and the only remedy is to remove the plants from the garden and discard them. As we pulled up some of my favorite roses, my heart was saddened. My fire for gardening has been dampened heavily. I need to be reignited, and maybe in the spring, something will reignite my love of gardening.

While losing roses is not a tragedy, we do deal with serious things that can take away our spirit—health issues, financial stress, loss of loved ones, and many more. Yet, there is always the hope of being reignited!

How do we reignite our inner soul again? Often, time just needs to pass. Then, there will be a moment when we feel that inner ember is still there. And just like that—the ember will spark a fire. Something or someone in our life triggers that little spark, and we begin to be excited about things again. This beautiful nurse was reignited by the people she was working with and the patients with whom she served every day. She was surrounded by people who made a difference in her life.

When we hit a roadblock or are discouraged, do we surround ourselves with the people who bring a spark to our life? Every word we say can change a life. It can be the spark that changes another or reignites their soul to begin again. I have challenged myself to look for opportunities to say something encouraging to the people I encounter. Even the smallest of comments may make a difference, so let's do it together! *—August 2018*

More Beautiful with Age

I celebrated another birthday this past weekend, and that always makes me stop and think about how fast time is passing. It's probably going at the same rate; it just feels faster as wrinkles and various "saggings" are more pronounced and seem to appear overnight. Just saying! I made the mistake of buying a makeup mirror that has 10X power. Mercy, I can see the cells in my skin! But in order to get the eyeliner close to my lashes, it was necessary. But it does reveal that my face could resemble the map of Canada very soon. I am the oldest child of three, and I always tell people I am the youngest, which drives my sister, Janice, totally nuts. She has guest blogged before, and I am sure you remember her. She is the baby. Another topic for another day.

A doctor said to me several years ago, as he was grimacing about his clients who love Botox, "Why can't you women just age gracefully? Put away the magnifying mirrors and be beautiful for the age you are!" As we talked, he said the movie stars who were considered glamorous and popular in the 1950s didn't have all these wonder drugs. They became more beautiful with age. I attributed it to Pond's Cold Cream. My grandmothers used that!

More beautiful with age . . . that is something to ponder. It is not just our physical appearance but our countenance and inner beauty that make us who we are. More beautiful with age is a lovely thought to dwell on. While we will all continue the fight against wrinkles, I have known some of the most physically beautiful women who were so hateful that there was no beauty. Our true beauty, or lack of it, comes from within.

Inner beauty is the kind that seeps from our heart to our face. Our eyes show it, our smile reveals it, and our face has a radiant look that can't be faked. That doesn't mean that we won't have hard times, but even through those times, we can be ourselves. I like to think that what we put in our mind grows in our heart. If we fill our thoughts with lovely moments and things that encourage us, we will see beauty grow in us. It will crowd out the negative that lurks everywhere today. We can bring encouragement to those who are in need of a loving word.

So, as I start another year of my life, I pray I will find things to fill my heart that will spill over into my words and expressions on my face that will be pleasing to those around me. But yes, I will color my hair and slather on the creams . . . some things will never change! *—October 2020*

CHERRY-PECAN CAKE

Makes 1 (8-inch) cake

2¼ cups unbleached cake flour
1½ cups granulated sugar
2 teaspoons baking powder
½ teaspoon kosher salt
¼ teaspoon baking soda
¾ cup unsalted butter, softened
¾ cup whole milk, room temperature
3 large egg whites, room temperature
3 tablespoons sour cream, room temperature
1½ teaspoons vanilla extract
Vanilla-Almond Buttercream (recipe follows)
1 cup finely chopped maraschino cherries, patted dry
½ cup finely chopped toasted pecans

1. Preheat oven to 350°. Spray 3 (8-inch) round cake pans with baking spray with flour. Line bottom of pans with parchment paper.
2. In the bowl of a stand mixer, whisk together flour, sugar, baking powder, salt, and baking soda by hand. Add butter; using the paddle attachment, beat at medium-low speed until butter is incorporated and mixture resembles coarse crumbs, about 2 minutes.
3. In a medium bowl, whisk together milk, egg whites, sour cream, and vanilla. With mixer on low speed, add one-third of milk mixture (about ⅔ cup) to flour mixture. Increase mixer speed to medium, and beat until light and fluffy, 1 to 2 minutes. Gradually add remaining milk mixture, beating until well combined and stopping to scrape sides of bowl. Divide batter among prepared pans (about 1½ cups).
4. Bake until a wooden pick inserted in center comes out clean, 20 to 30 minutes. Let cool in pans on wire racks for 10 minutes. Remove from pans, and let cool completely on wire racks.
5. In another medium bowl, stir together 3 cups Vanilla-Almond Buttercream, cherries, and pecans.
6. Level cooled cake layers, if desired. Place 1 cake layer on a serving plate. Spread half of cherry buttercream mixture on top. Top with second cake layer, and spread remaining cherry buttercream mixture on top. Top with remaining cake layer.
7. In a small bowl, reserve 1 cup Vanilla-Almond Buttercream. Spread remaining buttercream on top and sides of cake. Using an offset spatula, scrape excess frosting off sides of cake to smooth and expose cake layers, if desired. Refrigerate assembled cake for at least 15 minutes.
8. Transfer reserved buttercream to a pastry bag fitted with a medium open star piping tip (Ateco #826). Pipe buttercream on top of cake as desired. Cover and refrigerate for up to 3 days.

VANILLA-ALMOND BUTTERCREAM

Makes about 8 cups

2½ cups unsalted butter, softened
2 teaspoons kosher salt
7¾ cups confectioners' sugar
¾ cup heavy whipping cream
2¼ teaspoons almond extract
1¼ teaspoons vanilla extract

1. In the bowl of a stand mixer fitted with the paddle attachment, beat butter and salt at medium speed until smooth and creamy, 1 to 2 minutes. With mixer on low speed, add confectioners' sugar, 1 cup at a time, alternately with cream and extracts, beating until combined after each addition and stopping to scrape sides and bottom of bowl. Increase mixer speed to medium-high, and beat until pale and fluffy, 1 to 2 minutes. Use immediately.

Discovering Calm in Great Sorrow

There are weeks where you just can't seem to understand many things. This is one of those weeks. I have watched with great sorrow the accounts of two more mass shootings in our country.

I want to scream, "Stop it!" I have experienced the loss of friends and family through death, but never through an event like this. My mind can't comprehend being on the premises when something like this happens and witnessing shootings. It's hard enough to deal with a death of a loved one, but this—I can't even begin to imagine.

We are a nation that has lived through many tragedies like this, and we pull together. The days and months following 9/11 were a time of unity and compassion. We reached out to everyone to help bring a little bit of calm to a horrible time.

I look at things on a personal level and try to imagine what went wrong that a person felt shooting others was the answer. Did we miss something? Were we too busy to notice a cry for help? I don't have the answers. I wish I did.

Please let this serve as an encouragement to you that if you need someone to speak with about a loss or a difficult time in your life, please reach out. Sometimes just sharing with another person lightens the load and brings a little calm in your soul. A moment shared may be the turning point of your life. You are special to someone. You have great worth and great gifts to offer. When discouragement comes, it is only temporary, and it will pass. The passing of time gives us new perspective.

When I have the privilege of speaking at events, most of them women's events, I close with this thought that I want to share with you:

Right now, someone is thinking of you.
Someone wants to laugh with you.
Someone wants to hold your hand.
Someone wants to be the shoulder you cry on.
Someone wants to see your smile and hear your voice.
Right now, someone wants to give you a gift,
And someone thinks you are the gift!

Our lives have great worth. Live each day to the fullest, and when the sun goes down, rejoice that we lived another day.

If you need a person to share with and you don't have anyone, please contact me. I might not have the answer, but I do have a heart that will listen.

Love to you all. —*August 2019*

Am I an Encourager?

I have pondered this so many times this past week—am I an encourager?

We meet people all the time. Some just cross our paths, and some are part of our daily lives. I have noted that there are people who make us feel so loved and valued and then others who make us wish we had never been around them. The difference, I find, is in their ability to value and encourage others by simple little gestures.

Have you noticed that when someone comments on our outfit or new haircut, we immediately perk up? Or when someone belittles another, we wilt away. Developing habits of being an encourager is a practice, but it's one well worth pursuing. Kind thoughts aren't meant to be harbored only in our minds but to be shared. Now, I am not talking about flattery that has no substance but true caring and commenting. It takes effort to really notice and compliment one another. We are always moving at a fast pace, and slowing down enough to acknowledge others requires real concentration.

I love being around happy people—people who make my day better. Inevitably, we all deal with challenges and problems, so it's always refreshing to see a friend who chooses to look for the silver lining. As situations and seasons come and go, cling tightly to those friends.

Don't ever underestimate the power of the spoken word. Words laced with encouragement and positive recognition are life-changing. There is power in speaking them and receiving them. I am challenging myself today to be an encourager—to surround myself with people who bring out the best in me and others.

One day here at the office, one of our precious young employees left beautiful yellow roses on my desk without a note. I finally found out the giver, and I asked, "Why no name?" She responded: "I just wanted to brighten your day." Wow, that is powerful! She didn't want any recognition—just to brighten my day. And she certainly did!

Today and every day, I am going to notice more carefully, share kind thoughts often, and hopefully, just brighten someone's day. *—August 2018*

"The turns of life are unpredictable—
no one can know what is coming
tomorrow or this afternoon—but
how sweet it is to remember that our
faith is in a God who does know what
tomorrow holds and whose love for us
never wavers even the slightest bit."

Phyllis

Waiting Graciously

For those of you who know me, you know I hate to wait. Now, I can hear you saying, "Everyone has to wait." This is very true, but I like to keep moving. I found myself watching the microwave tick down and thought, "Please, hurry up!" A microwave that cooks in record time wasn't going fast enough for me. Really? Now, that's when I need a gut check on waiting.

Mom used to tell me: "A watched pot never boils." At the time, I knew she was trying to teach me patience and that things take time—usually more time than I wanted them to.

We have become an instant gratification society, haven't we? Things are so fast; it makes our heads spin, but it has become the new norm. Waiting is a lost art form. We just don't like to wait in lines, on the phone, in traffic, or in the kitchen when something fabulous is cooking. Probably because we can't control those minutes, they just must tick down on the clock—slowly.

Now, if it's something I really love doing, time flies. I don't notice time passing if I have a friend in the car while we are waiting on a red light or waiting for food in a restaurant.

Was I always like this? Or have I developed this unhealthy trait of impatience as I have aged? Who knows?

I have decided to really focus on waiting graciously, knowing I will fail often, but I am still going to try very hard. Sitting still in a restaurant or a doctor's office until my appointed time has come is something I will consciously try to master without getting antsy. Are you a calm person when you wait? —*September 2019*

Finding Courage in the Face of Obstacles

I love Winston Churchill's quote: "Success is not final, failure is not fatal: it is the courage to continue that counts."

Courage is something that many of us struggle with in the challenges of our lives. It is not uncommon for a disappointment or failure to knock the wind out of our sails, leaving us weak in our efforts to go forward. Courage is something that comes from within us and becomes weaker with each passing disappointment. That is why the part of the quote "failure is not fatal" is so uplifting.

Failures come in many forms. We often associate failure with a business loss or job that has been eliminated, and we feel we have failed. Neal and I traveled to Montana this past summer as I shared with you in an earlier post. One of the highlights for us was our morning coffee and breakfast at a tiny little place called The Coffee Pot Bakery Cafe. The little cabin was actually divided into two sections: the coffee shop, with its small tables and delightful homemade pastry offerings, and the pottery side, where the most beautiful handmade pottery was displayed for sale.

Upon inquiring, the owner came over to speak with us. She was just delightful as she shared her story of The Coffee Pot. She and her husband had moved to Montana to start over after losing a business. She said they came with the talents that they had and a desire to start over. She was a great cook, and he was a master potter. They came up with the idea of a little place where they could offer wonderful food to their guests. He made the wonderful pottery for the shop, and each customer was served on his beautiful creations.

As the demand for these marvelous serving pieces, mugs, and plates increased, he put a workshop in the back of the shop, and there he made beautiful pottery to sell. Today, they ship pottery all over the country. As customers pile in for their treats, they often leave with a lovely piece of pottery and a bakery box filled with delicious food.

The smile on her face was radiant as she told how God had blessed their talents and desire to start over after a failure. Her courage was inspiring to me. It wasn't easy, and it took hard work, but their courage to begin again was evident in her story. I came away with beautiful memories of our week there and the wonderful time we spent every morning at The Coffee Pot.

If you are struggling with starting over today, take courage. Find that inner strength that comes from God, and let it fill your heart and mind as you take one step at a time. The times in my life when I have experienced failure, I began with baby steps as I navigated my way forward.

Look at your talents and opportunities. Take inspiration from those around you and be strong. Each day brings a new journey. —*September 2015*

Treasuring Each Day

I think I have been sheltered now for 10 weeks. Since I'm at high risk with anemia, my family put the whammy on me early in this pandemic adventure.

During the first week, I thought, this is really great. Working from home and finishing up the sewing magazine for press would be fun. Challenging maybe but fun. Our teams are troupers, and they have done amazing work during this time. Creative people love interaction. Yes, that's me.

What have we learned during this time?

I can still cook. And cook. And cook. I have tried new recipes and cooked some of our favorites.

We lost a dear friend to the COVID-19 virus. That changed the world for us. Life is a treasured gift. Each day, we must look around us at the gifts God has given by putting special people in our lives. Have you told your best friend how much you love them?

Family time. We will look back on this pandemic as a time when our time was spent with the ones we love the most. Never would families spend this much time together. But what a gift. We will look back on this period and long for time together again, not under these circumstances but when the world gets busy again.

Mothers have had the most beautiful time to be with their children. Mothers have ceased to be taxi drivers and have had their children all to themselves. Some realized early on that this is a treasured period of time in life. It has been challenging with the schooltime moved to our homes. Keeping the children on track without instilling panic has been something to accomplish. Right now, we are wishing things to be like they were. When kids are grown, this will be a time remembered with great fondness.

A dear friend said something that I have thought about: "We didn't realize what a great life we had until it was gone." I miss hugging my grandchildren and grown children. I long for that to return quickly. When it comes to things that really matter, it is our precious people in our lives.

May God bless us all as we progress through the remainder of this time. May we be better people and learn from this pandemic. May each minute of every day be something we treasure. *—May 2020*

Not My Problem

Too often in life we become overly concerned about a problem that we cannot fix. You know what I mean. Your ideas and thoughts are much better than the route being taken, but at the end of the day, it doesn't matter.

I was grimacing one day about a change coming that no longer involved me, yet I had concerns. My dear friend held up three fingers and said, "Remember this?" The three fingers mean, "Not. My. Problem!" Wow, that was freeing to hear. Not My Problem . . . and I realized that no matter how much I agonized, there was nothing I could do or say to change the decision that had been made.

Not My Problem. Interesting thought. My friend was absolutely right! It was most certainly not my problem. So freeing, so liberating, and so accurate. How many times do we "borrow trouble," as my grandmother used to say? We get emotionally involved in issues that are outside of our sphere of influence. Yet, when we know those involved and can see a train wreck on the horizon, we can't help but be interested.

I am always open to listen when anyone has a predicament and they need to vent or share. Sometimes, it helps to have someone to talk to. I can always give ideas for possible solutions, but ultimately, I know the decisions that need to be made are not mine.

Sometimes, when I fret over a predicament, Neal will be the one to hold up three fingers. I am quickly reminded that it is Not My Problem. It is also freeing to hold up those three fingers to someone when they are trying to drag you into a conversation or ordeal where you don't belong.

It is setting boundaries for ourselves, isn't it? We can lose many nights of sleep worrying about things that we simply cannot change. We toss and turn, flip the pillow, and then ultimately wear ourselves out over a dilemma that is not ours to solve. Truly, this stems from how deeply we care about these people.

But remember the three fingers! Not My Problem. You will find a smile will be on your face, and you will sleep better knowing your limitations in a situation that's not yours to handle. *—June 2019*

Working Through Change

There's one thing that is certain in life: everything changes. I hate change. I love going to my favorite restaurant and knowing my favorite dish will be right on the menu, center column, fourth from the top. But the real springer? One day, I went there, and there was a new menu for the season. Oh no, change!

Why does change bother us? I realize some change is good, but most of us are happy where we are, doing exactly what we want to do. Change is unsettling.

With great humor, I watch the seating order in church. When a new couple comes in and sits down, the reaction from the people whose seat they have "taken" is hilarious. Not that they mind, but they have to move. Move? Oh my, everything looks different from another seat!

How do we accept change? That is the question we will all be asking ourselves for the rest of our lives. Sometimes, change is brought upon us, and there is nothing we can do. Change sometimes occurs by our decisions to change. And then, there is natural change that takes place as we age.

I have a marvelous, wonderful, talented, genius, young doctor whom I adore. He is younger than my sons. Going for a visit is actually delightful because he lets you know everything is going to be fine, even when you are discouraged. We were going through the vitamins and meds that I am taking, and he said the most amazing thing: "This vitamin has all kinds of great stuff for a woman your age."

A WOMAN MY AGE? Are you kidding? I could blend in with the 40-year-olds . . . well, maybe not. Without thinking, I held up my fist and said, "If you say that again, I will show you what a woman my age can do!" He about fell off his stool laughing. It was a funny moment. I am old enough to be his mother, and so, that's our standing joke—for a woman my age.

Change is here. It's happening, and we have to embrace it. The good news is everyone ages at the same time. Have you noticed that? Days aren't going any faster for me than for you. In my mind, I will always be 30; my mother will always be 50, and I don't look any different than I did in high school. Well, that's in my mind. But I can tell you this: my shoes from high school still fit perfectly. *—January 2018*

Why I'll Always Remember Dixie Carter

There are people who come into your life and make a real impact, leaving you with wonderful memories of special times together. Such was my experience with Dixie Carter. The late actress is most fondly known for her role as the sassy Julia Sugarbaker in the television show *Designing Women*.

I met her several years ago at Southern Lady Celebration, an event hosted by our company. She was our honored guest and awarded Southern Lady of the Year. Dixie told stories of her childhood in rural Tennessee and delighted our audience. Dixie once

sang for her mother on an episode of the show, and she recounted how it thrilled her mother. Dixie had a beautiful voice. When she finished her presentation, she asked me to come to the stage and sing "Amazing Grace" with her.

As I walked up, I was really unnerved; I play the piano but never sing in public, much less on the stage with Dixie Carter. As we sang, the audience rose to their feet and sang with us. The overwhelming emotion of that evening will last a lifetime for me. We kept in touch and had opportunities to visit several times during the next few years. I loved our friendship, and she always had the most encouraging, uplifting things to say.

I called Dixie one day and told her of a friend of mine whose daughter, Brynn, wanted to be an actress and asked if she would recommend an agent. She said she would do even better than that—she would take "Miss Brynn" to lunch. They met at a café in Hollywood, and Brynn's life was changed forever. Dixie opened her heart to a beautiful young lady who experienced the vivacious Dixie Carter who had become my friend.

When Dixie called to tell me that she was very ill and dying, I couldn't believe it. We had talked only a short while before about her new, delightful role on *Desperate Housewives* as a plotting, cranky, old lady. But that day, her call was somber. After her passing, I think back on her taking time to share her family, her faith, and her love of life with people she encountered. This tremendously famous lady loved life. And amid her intense schedule, she took time to change lives along the way, including a young Miss Brynn.

Greatness is found in the words that we speak from our hearts to encourage and affirm our friends and family. I will always remember Dixie's beautiful smiles, her Southern drawl, and her love of life. I am blessed to have called her my friend and to have shared a small part of her life. She will always be missed, and my life is enriched having known her. *—April 2014*

Meeting Life's Challenges

Dealing with challenges in life is never what we dream of spending our energy on. I find myself thinking, "Really—another obstacle?" I would rather be doing something fun!

Challenges often mean something consistent in our lives, in one way or another, is changing. With every shift in our normal comes a new decision to make. Now, I much prefer the method of "ignore it, and it will go away," but that never really solves anything long-term. This oh-so-tempting method provides momentary relief, but I find that the problem is not truly solved, and eventually, I will have to tend to it.

There is a saying: "What doesn't kill you makes you stronger." Do challenges make us stronger, more resilient, or tougher? I don't know for sure. But when the emotions settle and we set our minds to working through things, there is always some sort of relief on the other side.

I love finding little bits of inspiration and encouragement from observing the people I interact with in my daily life. One recent example is an experience I had at the doctor's office.

My doctor (the one who told me I was in that age group . . . yep, that one) is working on unraveling the cause of my anemia. I am a medical mystery. Though this tasks him, my doctor assures me that he will get to the bottom of it. And I have no doubt he will. He rises to the occasion no matter the circumstances!

There are times in our lives when we are too exhausted to take on the task at hand—too burned-out for problem-solving. But, friends, the good news is that trials produce perseverance. Our inner strength is there, even when we feel it's not.

Just like a garden, we must be pruned and trimmed in order to grow. And sometimes, that pruning isn't the most pleasant process.

Today, you may be facing health issues, family issues, work issues, or any change in your life. These challenges take time and calm thinking.

Don't give up or be so discouraged that you lose your way. Take it one day at a time, committing to prayer and stillness. Share your situation with a friend or family member. It lightens your load and strengthens you.

I am smiling today because of this beautiful reminder in Psalm 121:1–2 (KJV): "I will lift up mine eyes unto the hills, from whence cometh my help. My help cometh from the LORD, which made heaven and earth."

This Bible verse came to me while I was sitting on my porch having coffee. How thankful I am for truths such as this—that we always have the very best helper at our side. *—September 2018*

On Etiquette, Home & Entertaining

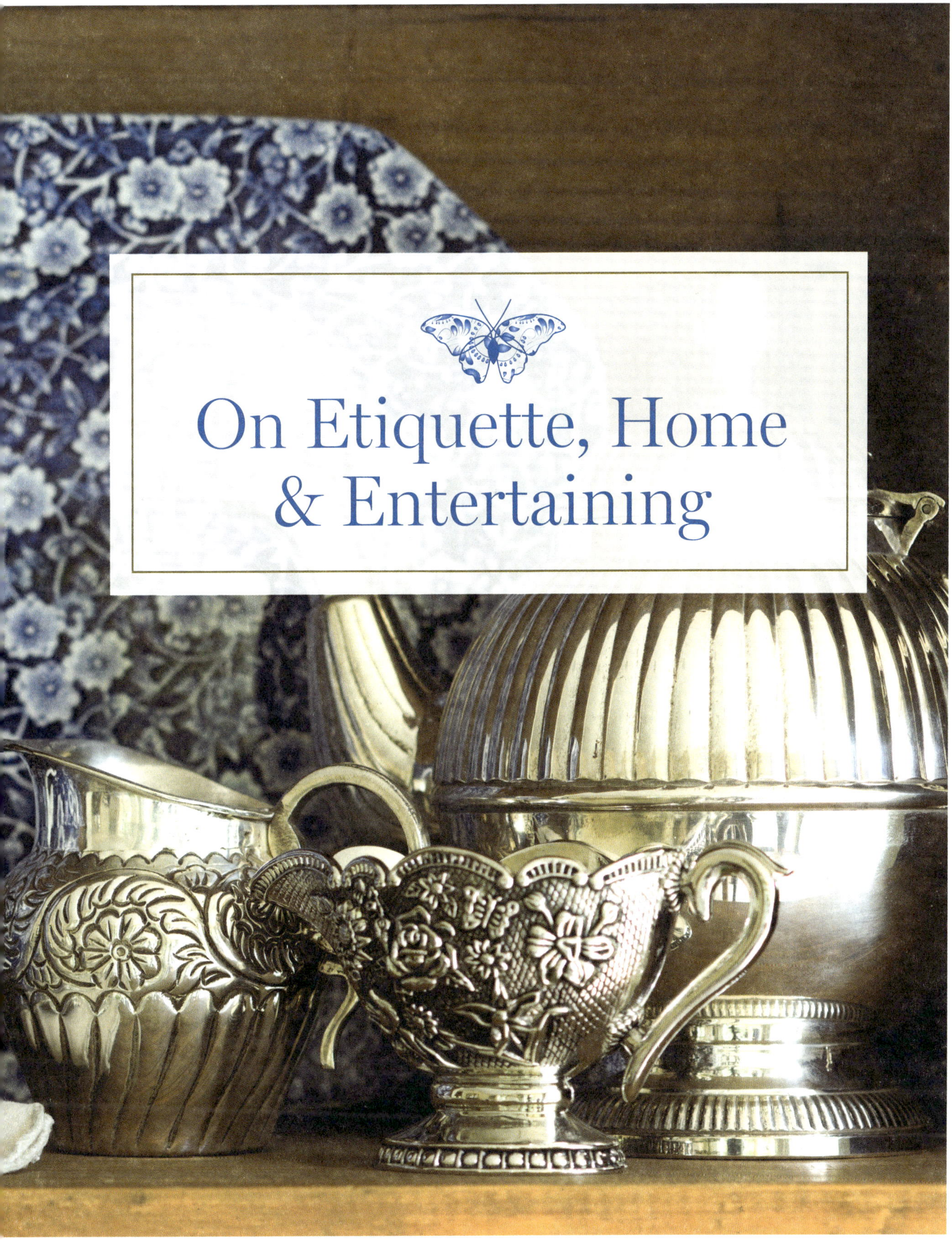

LOVING SUPPORT

DEAR PHYLLIS, I HOPE THIS LETTER FINDS YOU IN A PLACE of peace and comfort, surrounded by the warmth and love you so generously gave to those around you. As I sit down to write, I find myself reflecting on the many ways you touched my life with your kindness, humor, and unwavering support.

From the very beginning, you welcomed me into your life with open arms and an open heart. Your love was not just a feeling but a tangible gift, one that was expressed through countless thoughtful gestures and memorable moments. I still cherish the way you would light up when we went out for dinner on my birthday, celebrating with such joy and enthusiasm. Those dinners were more than just meals; they were a testament to the deep bond we shared and the respect we had for one another.

Your intelligence and wit were always so refreshing. Conversations with you were never mundane; they were filled with insight, laughter, and a genuine curiosity about life. I loved how we could talk about our businesses, understanding the challenges and triumphs that come with running one. It was in these moments that I felt a deep sense of camaraderie and respect for you, knowing that we both knew the hard work and dedication required to build something from the ground up.

Your ability to entertain and bring people together was truly remarkable. I fondly remember the beautiful wedding you hosted for us at your home, overlooking the bluff and adorned with a spectacular array of flowers. It was a day of magic and love, made even more special by your meticulous care and attention to detail. You had a unique talent for creating spaces where people felt cherished and celebrated, and your home was always a place of warmth and joy.

One of the things I'll always treasure is how you were the first person I wanted to share good news with. Your excitement and genuine happiness for me were always a source of comfort and encouragement. You made me feel like a part of your family, loving me as if I were your own son, and for that, I am eternally grateful.

Phyllis, your legacy is one of love, laughter, and unwavering support. You made every gathering special, every conversation meaningful, and every moment together a cherished memory. Though we may not have you with us in person, your spirit and the impact you've had on my life will always remain.

Thank you for being the incredible person you were and for loving me so deeply. I am blessed to have known you and to have been a part of your life.

—Stephen Hart Hoffman, son-in-law

Stephen Hart Hoffman

Gift Giving and Receiving

I don't know about you, but I am always overwhelmed when a friend brings me a little token of our friendship. Receiving is usually difficult for me, as I prefer to be in the giving role, but it is wonderful to be remembered.

One-of-a-kind ideas for hostess gifts are one thing I really struggle with. I am always looking for something unique to give instead of the traditional items of wine, flowers, or candy. I recently took a potted plant to a friend in hopes that she would love it for her garden. Another gift that is fun to give is a small book. A piece of vintage china is a lovely and unique gift to give as well. The important thing is to give yourself in a small, simple way.

Being remembered is an endearing thing. For those of you who have sent me things you have made, poems you have written, and letters of encouragement, thank you. I read every post you place on Ribbon, and each one is a gift from you. Share your love today with someone special. *—June 2016*

Total Dessert Disaster?

My staff always likes for me to talk about a total bust, something that really messed up despite my best-laid plans. Truth is usually stranger than fiction, and certainly, in my case, that is true.

Long before there even was a Hoffman Media and the magazines we publish, there was me who read everything under the sun that had to do with homes, cooking, and entertaining. Cooking and recipe ideas were my favorites. Now, I am the gutsy one in the family who always tries new recipes on my guests rather than going with the tried-and-true.

I was hosting a family dinner and decided to try a fancy, new dessert. You bake a two-layer cake of your choice and then, while your cake layers are cooling, you take your cake pans and fill them with semi-melted ice cream and refreeze. Then right before you serve it, you stack it, alternating layers of ice cream and cake. It was a beautiful photo in the magazine where I found the recipe, and I knew that I would score extra points for this one. Every layer was perfect, and I knew mine would be, too.

When the night came and the family was gathered, I was greatly anticipating the premiere of my dessert masterpiece. After the entrées were finished and it was time for dessert, I excused myself to the kitchen to assemble the cake that I would then bring out for all to see before I sliced it.

It was a total disaster. I placed the first layer of cake on the cake plate and then the first layer of ice cream on top. Then, the landslide began! I was trying to hold the ice cream in place while placing the second layer of cake on top, hoping this would stop the slide. Oh no, it made it worse! Every layer of ice cream was lopsided, and the cake layers were not level either.

I was standing there with a mudslide of melting ice cream and soggy cake. So, I found my trifle dish and crumbled everything into the dish. I found a bottle of chocolate syrup and drizzled it on the top. I rushed the new creation through the dining room and then back to the kitchen, where I very quickly served it up in bowls.

Everyone loved the new trifle and wanted the recipe. Go figure. *—June 2016*

Note: The pictured dessert is not the disastrous treat in question.

Dinner Etiquette: Keeping the Conversation Light

It's very uncomfortable being at dinner when, out of nowhere, a topic unsuitable for discussion at the table is introduced. What do you do? Well, the old Southern rule of table topics is this: no religion, no sex, and no politics. (Today, we could certainly add more to that list.) And my favorite rule is: don't repeat gossip!

Dinner should be light and enjoyable, and the talk around the table should be entertaining and conversational. Oftentimes, we find ourselves in awkward situations. What one finds amusing is not always amusing to others; or worse, a topic of great controversy is introduced. How do we stop that train wreck?

We have all been there when a question or comment is made that totally stops conversation and then ultimately puts a damper on an evening. A minister's wife gave me the best advice once, as she was always being put in the middle of such situations. She said when a person makes a statement hoping for a response, she always responds, "Well . . ."

For example: I think the choir was really bad today. "Well . . ." Her hair color is really awful, don't you think? "Well . . ." I will be glad when she retires. "Well . . ."

You are neither agreeing nor disagreeing with a comment, and it usually gives you the opportunity to change the subject to something more pleasant.

Table talk should be a family time for sharing positives, successes, and triumphs in our lives. It should never be a place for an argument, budget concerns, or scolding of a child's grades or school issues. Those discussions should always take place in private.

What do you do when you find yourself in an uncomfortable situation? First, change the subject, if you can, by telling a funny story or sharing something humorous. Second, ask a question to someone at the table about themselves that will totally lead talk in a different direction. Third, sometimes, being quiet and not commenting is the best course of action. Silence will many times squelch a conversation quickly. You can only have a conversation when two are talking.

I love table time when funny stories of our days are shared or when our grandchildren share things from their perspective. Always give children your undivided attention. They need to know that they are just as important as anyone at the table and that their comments are welcome.

I want people who come to my home to remember the fun times of laughter and lighthearted chatter around the table. I can remember meals at my grandmother's house when all the girl cousins would share stories of school, current loves, and bad hair days. Everything ended in giggles, and those are the memories that I cherish.
—May 2016

Teaching Kids Table Manners

I have two of the most animated grandchildren in the world. Amelia and Hays are so much fun and so full of life. For those of you who have grandchildren, you understand! I am often asked about etiquette for children and specifically about table manners.

My, what a subject: table manners for children. When I was growing up, table manners were expected everywhere we went, and it started in our home. My mother, Mimi to the grandchildren, was just as mischievous as us kids, so Dad had his hands full. At 88, she is still the same. That's why my grandchildren want to sit with Mimi at the table; they know good times will abound. And that's what it's all about: enjoying every moment together around the table.

We had happy times around the table, but we were expected to behave. We were led by example, and that is truly the way most children are taught. There are courses children can attend where the basics are taught, but children typically imitate what they see. Our pastor makes a great statement when he dedicates babies: "Children will seldom listen, but they will always be watching." Well, if that doesn't hit home, nothing does.

My grandchildren know when they come to our home, we always sit down at the table to eat. I ask them questions as we eat, such as, "Where is your napkin placed?" or "If you don't like something, what do you do?" Their answers are always funny, especially when you discuss things you don't like to eat. But it makes them think.

When we go out to eat, as we are driving to the restaurant, I talk about how wonderful it is to dine out but that we must always think about those around us. Not only is it important that we have a wonderful meal but so must other families seated near us.

I gave them an example of an experience Neal and I had not long ago. We were dining out, and at a nearby table, a young child (but old enough to know better) was constantly screaming and running around. You could see heads turn and eyes roll and shoulders rise, but the parents were totally oblivious. In my attempt to solidify this lesson, I ask my grandchildren to find the most well-behaved child in the restaurant. It is amazing that they will observe bad manners and good manners.

Our table should be a place of fellowship and sharing life. Conversations and fun moments will always be treasured. Consistency in combining manners with fun will result in enjoyment. As children age, occasions will call for more instruction, but live in the moment and let the smiles abound. *—March 2016*

"Table manners were a must at our house. Dad loved the time spent around the table and insisted that we put forth our best. Little did we know he was preparing us for our adult lives of meeting people in our careers. 'You need to extend your hand when I introduce you and respond with nice to meet you,' he would say. It was important to him that when we were introduced we knew how to respond."

Phyllis

Hospitality Trays 101

It is often the simplest of gestures that let people know you care. Hospitality trays might sound elevated and fancy, but they could not be any easier to put together! Create this special experience for your guests just once, and you'll do it again and again when you see how delighted they are.

Having one of these trays set out for overnight guests stems from the genuine concern for your guest's comfort, and it's the ultimate nod to Southern hospitality. Plus, it gives off a "bed-and-breakfast" vibe in such a fun way.

Hospitality trays have three basic components (other than the tray itself). All you need is a pot of tea or coffee or a carafe of ice water, a small snack or two, and serve ware. Flowers are wonderful touch as well, but if you are in a pinch, the tray will still come together beautifully without them.

Remember, we are keeping the food simple! For young people, you can add their favorite packaged snacks. If you have the time to make homemade treats for your tray, that is wonderful. But fresh fruit or scones or cookies from the bakery will do just fine. *—February 2019*

Unique Centerpieces

It can be a challenge to keep your home's décor fresh and exciting, especially when entertaining. I can easily find myself falling into a rut with tablescapes. One way I have found to challenge myself and keep my skills sharp is to repurpose unconventional items as unique centerpieces for my table. Some of you may remember my post about using tea canisters for flower arranging.

Cream pitchers and sugar bowls are pieces that I also love to use and always have around. If I'm not serving coffee, then I will use the cream pitcher and sugar bowl from the pattern of dishes that I set the table with to hold small arrangements. In summer, I like to scatter fresh produce with lively hues on the table like heirloom tomatoes. Add lanterns or rustic boxes, and remember to select your flowers with care, choosing a seasonal mix from your yard or even the grocery store for the freshest display.

One of my absolute favorite items I have used as a centerpiece is a high-heel shoe. You can place the flowers in a small container inside the shoe, creating an attention-grabbing vignette without taking up too much space.

Using unorthodox items for centerpieces is a wonderful way to use your treasures that may be gathering dust in your cabinets. Search estate sales and antiques shops for unique centerpieces as well—you'll be surprised at what you can find. No matter how you end up decorating your table, let your creativity and style shine through. That will make anything beautiful. *—August 2016*

Finding a Quiet Spot at Home

When I was growing up, my mother, who is a very patient woman, would look at me and quote the Bible verse that says, "Be still, and know that I am God." I would think in my mind, "I am too busy to be still." Being still simply was not the choice of this young person.

Even more amazing is when I hear an exasperated young mother tell her child to go to "time-out." Understand, I am not disagreeing with the young mother, but now that

I'm grown, I would just love for someone to tell me that I am going to "time-out." I think I would ask, "How long may I stay?"

When I have moments that I can just be still and have some quiet time at home, it gives me time to let my mind rest. I try to sit in my favorite chair with a cup of tea and just be quiet. Most of us find that when we give our minds time to rest, we start making mental notes of everything we must do that day. And before you know it, we are right back where we started.

How do we relax and renew our souls? First, as Mom said, be still. Find a beautiful place that you love and make that your place of relaxation; it may be in your garden, on the porch, or in your favorite chair. We must then disconnect. Turn off the cell phones and devices that will interrupt our time.

Don't be afraid of quiet. I love to sit on my porch with morning coffee and listen to the amazing sounds of nature on any given day. The birds are unusually musical, and the breeze blowing through the leaves sings its own song.

The biggest challenge in being alone is renewing our minds. I find that if I start thinking of all the things I cherish and love, my mind doesn't return to "the list" of upcoming responsibilities. I think of my grandchildren and what they may be doing at school. Remembering beautiful moments in my life is always restorative. Creative things I want to do in the upcoming days also fill my mind, and I find that my creative juices start flowing.

"Be still, and know that I am God" is still a verse that I cling to. I understand it now more than ever. Today, find your quiet place. —*September 2015*

Personal Notes

I love people who are encouragers! I have a friend who sends cards at just the right time, and I find myself thinking, "I wish I had done that." It is amazing how a note of encouragement or a letter will transform your day.

I tend to be someone who moves way too fast in an already fast-paced world. My mind thinks that I should send a handwritten note to a person who has accomplished something or just needs a little encouragement, but then, I become distracted. Now mind you, I am fully stocked with beautiful stationery, pens, and stamps in the right-hand drawer of my desk. Even so, many times, I still let the moment pass.

I have a new plan. First thing in the morning when I get to my desk, I will write appropriate notes before I get my day started. If I don't, then I will never get back to it. In the quiet of the morning, I can best collect my thoughts and words.

There is something very therapeutic about seeing ink flow across the paper and hearing the sound of the pen as each letter is formed. Expressing gratitude, condolences, and congratulations gives an opportunity to reach out to a friend to let them know they are remembered.

I know how I feel when I get a letter, card, or note. I put that envelope aside, and after the bills and other less personal mail are read and handled, the ceremony of opening the handwritten correspondence begins. Each word resonates in my mind as I read it.

Encouragement comes in many forms. The important thing is for the person to know they were thought of fondly and remembered for a moment in our day. In the days ahead, I want to become an encourager and make a difference with a special note. —*October 2015*

Dearest Angelin
Wishing you the mos
beautiful birthda
thank
you

Postcards

It always makes my day when I open my mailbox to a handwritten letter from a friend. I have always loved writing and receiving notes, and I intend to keep handwritten correspondence a priority in my life. With the speed of technology, it is becoming more and more rare to receive words written by hand. There is still a simple and beautiful way to maintain this art: postcards!

I vividly remember the first time I was introduced to postcards. Growing up, my siblings and I rarely had a babysitter, but when we did, it was always our sweet neighbor, Mrs. Trainor. The first time she came to our house, she had two shoeboxes tucked under her arm. We were immediately intrigued and began speculating as to what treasure was hidden within these mysterious boxes. When she opened the boxes, we saw that they were filled to the brim with postcards. For the next few hours, my siblings and I sat with her, admiring the beautiful pictures and designs of each postcard.

Each postcard was from a special place and featured an accompanying story from Mrs. Trainor. When she left for the day, we felt as if we had traveled both the country and the world with her. Each time she went on a trip, she made sure to purchase at least one postcard to add to her collection. These tokens allowed her to remember each of her many trips for years to come.

Mrs. Trainor's tradition is an easy one that you can adopt. Postcards are an inexpensive and unique souvenir that can be purchased at many destinations. Taking a minute to write a short note on a postcard is a quick and meaningful way to share your travels with friends and family. Postcards are also a great way to introduce children to the lost art of writing letters by hand. In the midst of our daily hustle and bustle, let's be intentional about reclaiming authentic communication, one postcard at a time. *—August 2016*

How To Be the Perfect Holiday Guest

I love holidays and look forward to all gatherings of friends and family. I have been asked by several people to write some etiquette suggestions for being a well-mannered guest for holiday celebrations. Now, I do not profess to be the holiday etiquette queen, but I have learned a few interesting things in my life. Watching guests arrive and seeing the reactions of hostesses have always been a source of fun at dinner parties and luncheons.

So, here are some humorous but true thoughts on being the perfect guest:

The perfect guest always arrives on time.
This is a biggy. Being late to any event where food has been prepared and timed for the appointed hour really drives a hostess mad. If you are going to be late, you probably know about it before the time to be there. Call, let the hostess know, and tell her to go ahead without you. Then, jump in at the course they are on when you arrive.

The perfect guest leaves the cell phone off the table and puts it away until after the party.
If you are expecting a call, excuse yourself from the table and check your phone. Using your cell phone at the table is rude and totally unacceptable. One lady I know has a cell phone box that she keeps at the door, and each guest is asked to place their phone in it. I have often wanted to see one phone ring and eight people dive for the box! Common sense should prevail.

The perfect guest does not bring another guest.
End of comment.

The perfect guest usually brings a hostess gift.
However, do not bring food unless the dinner is "covered dish," where all guests are bringing food. There is nothing more irritating than when a guest shows up with a dish of food and expects it to be served at the meal. The hostess has planned the menu and isn't expecting any additions. If you feel you must take food (being from

the South, I know some just can't help it, bless their hearts!), then take something for the family to eat at another time. If you want to make a dessert, then clear it with the hostess before you begin making it. If she says she has everything handled, take her at her word. Great hostess gifts include flowers (already in a container), wine, candy, or a book—something to show appreciation.

The perfect guest knows when to go home.

There have been times when I look back and remember dinners where I was still talking to a guest long after everyone had left and wishing in my heart that she knew how badly my feet hurt from standing and cooking. Not to mention that after guests leave, the cleaning begins. So, leave when it's over. If it's your very best friend, then tell her to take her shoes off, put on an apron, and help.

The perfect guest writes a thank-you note.

Just a few simple lines written by hand mean so much to the hostess who prepared a lovely meal for you.

Have fun, enjoy your next holiday occasion, whether it's a Fourth of July barbecue or Thanksgiving feast, and remember to be the perfect guest! *—November 2015*

How To Be the Perfect Hostess

Did you know we have some expert hostesses in our midst? After reading your responses to my last etiquette post, I can only imagine how wonderful being a guest at one of your homes would be! Your thoughts on how to be a perfect hostess are too good not to share.

Graciously opening your home to others is as much about your state of mind as it is about the food you serve and the décor you prepare. You have provided such good reminders that thoughtfulness and consideration are at the heart of hospitality. If you are comfortable and at ease, your guests will feel free to relax and enjoy themselves.

We all know that having guests means that the unexpected will happen. There's no amount of perfect planning that can eliminate the accidental spill on the table or the

guest who couldn't avoid being late. But a sound mind going into the party allows you to approach the unexpected with grace and good humor. Don't be afraid to laugh, friends!

As we approach the holiday season, here are some handy tips for being a good hostess that Ribbon readers offered:

• Remember the Golden Rule: "Do unto others as you would have others do unto you." If everyone would follow that rule, then every party would be a smashing love fest, and everyone would have a wonderful time and be filled with gratitude.

• Greet your guests at the door. A warm and sincere greeting goes a long way to set the tone for the evening.

• A good hostess is thoughtful and introduces guests to each other, pointing out something interesting about the guests or what they have in common so that when she leaves them to join other guests, they have a starting point of conversation. Thoughtfulness also includes being organized, cheerful, and relaxed. Your guests come to see you and have a good time; a nervous wreck of a hostess does not make guests feel good!

• Make sure comfort and convenience are assured with details like coasters on all unprotected surfaces or extra toilet tissue visible in bathrooms as well as facial tissue available. Don't display very fragile cherished items in places where they could easily be knocked over by children or adults in overcrowded rooms.

• Accommodate special diets whenever possible. Try to find out what your guests enjoy eating and if there are any food allergies or problems. Many people these days adhere to vegan, gluten-free, or lactose-free diets. It is a good idea to label all dishes so your guests know what is in them.

• Offer a simple favor for guests to depart on a happy note. Have a gift basket placed somewhere near the door with specially wrapped soaps, a small photo frame, ornaments at holidays, candies, or homemade gifts. No one leaves without a little something.

I hope that all of you enjoy your role as a hostess. Considering the thoughtful ideas you've shared here, I'm sure your homes will be full of joy this season and year-round.
—December 2015

ROOMS
A HOUSE IN THE COUNTRY
FARROW&BALL THE ART OF COLOR

Building Our House

You should think about creating a space of tranquility for yourself. If you are considering remodeling or redecorating, design a space that takes you away from the noise of everyday life. When Neal and I were building our house, we designed it to be a calming escape, a retreat.

Living rooms should be both comfortable and welcoming, and that's how I designed mine. Blue and white make such a classic color combination, so I chose the lovely duo for my great room and, really, for the whole house. I just love the great room's high vaulted ceilings and the tall wainscot paneling on the walls! My black grand piano sits by the window so I can play and feel like I am in my garden, which is usually in bloom with seasonal flowers.

The large windows give a great view of our front garden and allow natural light to flow in, making the space crisp and bright. The room is so large. We always tell our guests, "You are in the living room, music room, and dining room . . . It's all in the great room."

One of the main focal points of the living area is the vintage mahogany mantel, where I love to display fresh flowers in my blue-and-white china vases. The mantel is from an old home in Birmingham, Alabama, and it's thrilling to have a piece of history in our home.

Across from the mantel, my living room connects to the kitchen with a large, stone-lined opening. A reclaimed header beam from an 1860s factory in Mississippi sits on top. I wanted my kitchen to be a part of our living room so that when we all gather, we feel as though we are in one room.

My kitchen is my happy place. My cooktop faces the great room so I can enjoy conversations and hear the latest news when we have company. While I finish preparing a meal, I can still be a part of the conversation. I love the extra-wide counter chair—it's a great place to sit and talk while Neal or I cook, and it is just perfect for my grandchildren.

Being short, I opted out of overhead cabinets and, instead, built a large pantry where food and dishes are stored. The two cabinets in my kitchen where my blue-and-white dishes are displayed were designed to look like antique cabinets. They are actually new cabinets with seeded glass panes that make them look really old. When you are remodeling or planning your space, think about what works for you. Being able to reach things comfortably makes cooking fun!

Nestled behind my kitchen, the central pantry contains everything I need while cooking delicious meals. The purpose of my pantry is storage of and easy access to items essential to the kitchen. My pantry keeps food, dishes and china, glassware, and crystal organized and accessible.

The antique rolling pins, wooden cheese boxes, and breadboards serve as décor. Surrounding yourself with things you love is always a great starting point for decorating. The old-fashioned plate racks allow ample display areas for plates that are changed seasonally. Other cherished items find perfect spots on the display shelves.

When planning the house, Neal and I agreed that the main bedroom suite needed to be serene and relaxing with special attention to the bath. I paired powdery blue with white to give a refreshing and lightweight feel to the room. Not only do the windows framing the bathtub provide a beautiful backdrop, but they also let natural sunlight in, complementing the colors.

The galley bathroom style is perfect for us—Neal has his area, and I have mine. It was important that the storage was a pullout scheme; even the trash can slides right out—no more digging inside cabinets!

Sometimes, just a new coat of paint is all you need to refresh your home. Sometimes, you may have to do a little more. No matter how big the project, make each room your own and surround yourself with things you love. *—September 2017 to March 2018*

This tour of the home that Phyllis and Neal built in 2017 was done in several posts over six months. Here, we give you the highlights of Mom's thoughts and advice on building or renovating a home. —Brian and Eric

Planting Roots in Our New Home

Many of you have been so gracious to write and ask about the move into our new home (aka life apart from Sister!), which began in May. We are still unpacking strange boxes of unknown contents. So, it's like receiving a really interesting Christmas present from a distant relative.

One of my favorite things about our new home is my garden. You have to walk through my garden to get to the front door, a concept our architect suggested and we immediately loved.

Neal and I love raised beds because they are easy to maintain. I have a total dislike for getting on the ground to plant flowers, and this is perfect for me. We wanted an English garden and cottage look for our house, and the stone façade was the perfect choice. The over mortar technique is one that I have studied in English cottages for years. I am sure when those older cottages were built, it was for warmth that the joints between the bricks were completely sealed. I love the look and wanted to replicate it as close as possible with limestone colors in gray and brown.

We selected a synthetic slate to re-create the vintage look for the roof, but with modern technology and benefits. I love the texture, and everyone stops us and asks where we found the old slate.

Our garden gate is very special as it belonged to Neal's grandmother. He laughs and says he has moved that gate for years and finally it has a home. Stephen and Brian, two of our sons, gave us the fountain for Christmas this year. They wanted to give us something for the house, and this is the perfect fountain for my garden.

I feel like I am in England when I go to my garden. There is something tranquil about watering flowers and picking beautiful blossoms in the early morning light. I am adding roses and other favorite flowers gradually. I even found a *Downton Abbey* rose called 'Anna's Promise' (named for character Anna Bates) and just had to add it to my garden.

My garden is winding down for the summer as August heat has taken its toll, but in just a few weeks, I will be planting fall bulbs and additional roses. I think it would be fun to get a flower plant or bulb from friends and name them. I mean, Anna Bates is there, why not! *—August 2017*

"Paula and I have walked many steps together and have shared so much of our lives."

Phyllis

My Friend Paula Deen

Come one, come all, y'all!" as my good friend Paula Deen would say. Gathering around the dinner table for home-cooked family meals is one of the best things about our Southern lifestyle.

One of my favorite mealtime memories is when Neal and I had dinner with Paula and her husband Michael right in her kitchen. Originally, we invited them out to dinner, but she said she was happiest in her kitchen with family and friends. Paula glowed with delight as she put her freshly cooked food on the table, and we just went crazy tasting all the delicious dishes and her scrumptious biscuits. Neal will never be the same!

Truly, one of the most wonderful days of my life was when I met Paula. She had been writing for our *Taste of the South* magazine, and I watched her show religiously, but meeting her in person changed my life and the life of our company. Paula was our 2004 Southern Lady of the Year for our magazine, *Southern Lady*. I knew that people loved her, and from the response we had to her features in our magazines, I just knew that she needed her own magazine.

On the final day of the Celebration event in Destin, Florida, I sat down with Paula and presented her with a mock cover for a new magazine, *Cooking with Paula Deen*. She laughed and said, "No one wants to read about me." But we knew they would! She has been part of Hoffman Media since that first issue in 2005. By the fourth issue in, we were printing 1,000,000 copies. Yes, Paula, your readers love you! I wish I had a pan of her biscuits right now!—*February 2019*

Forty Years of Friendship

Years ago, I met Susan Gravely, the founder and owner of the Italian tableware company Vietri. Warm, kind, and funny, she is a delightful Southern lady if ever there was one. We have so much in common, and we became best friends. This year (2023), Susan and I are both celebrating a very special anniversary: we started our respective companies exactly 40 years ago. What a milestone! Susan has supported and encouraged me tirelessly as the Hoffman Media team and I have grown the business over the decades, and I've been privileged to do the same for her. Vietri's wonderful, often colorful china patterns have graced the pages of several of our magazines for years. From Vietri's beginnings to its huge success, I have loved watching the company become a worldwide favorite.

Susan's love of Italy, where Vietri's wares are designed and crafted, shines through in everything she does. Her book, *Italy on a Plate*, is beyond fabulous. Not only is it full of delicious recipes from her travels, but she also introduces us to local friends who have become special to Vietri's story and her personal story.

I love the story of how their business, Vietri, was birthed and how it continues to grow.

The Gravely sisters grew up in North Carolina, where porches wrap around the house, lightning bugs illuminate the night sky, entertaining is a way of life, and visitors are always welcome—especially around the dinner table. Susan and Frances remember well the careful preparation behind a special evening, and they were often asked, as most children are, to help set the table. Little did they know that very chore would turn into their life's passion.

Their business story starts with a magical trip to Italy in 1983. Susan, Frances, and their mother, Lee, headed first to the Amalfi Coast where they checked into the Il San Pietro di Positano hotel. During lunch at the hotel, the three women found themselves captivated by the hotel's colorful, handcrafted dinnerware. They immediately arranged to meet the artisans of the dinnerware at a nearby factory in the town of Vietri sul Mare. Their time at the small, bustling factory left them enchanted. Susan, Frances, and Lee were so taken by the Italian artisans' craftsmanship that they ended up spending three days with them, watching as they painted, glazed, and fired each piece by hand.

A special friendship developed between the talented Italians and the charming Southern women. Soon, they returned home with an array of "mix-and-match" pieces featuring whimsical cows, horses, rams, and fish—the collection that would become known as Campagna, Vietri's flagship dinnerware. The trio named their company Vietri as a tribute to the town where it all began and a play on the phrase *tre vite*, Italian for "three lives."

"The first container arriving in North Carolina is a memory I will never forget," says Susan, who with her mother, sister, and several friends unpacked the container. "We opened every piece and counted it by hand. The next morning, March 24, 1984, we shipped our very first order to our very first account: Neiman Marcus. They have been an account ever since!"

That was 40 years ago, and in the time since, Vietri has become the largest American importer of handcrafted Italian tableware and home décor products, working with multiple factories throughout Italy. A leader in design, craftsmanship, and customer service, the Vietri brand both complements the American lifestyle and celebrates all that is irresistibly Italian: a love of life, people, nature, and good living.
—May 2023

AROUND THE TABLE

MOM WAS THE CONSUMMATE HOST IN OUR HOME. Some of my fondest memories from high school, college, and on into when I started my first job were of Mom cooking dinner for my friends and roommates. She loved "taking care" of us and wanted us to be properly fed.

Given that she was a mother to boys, Mom knew how to please the crowd with wonderful and hearty dishes such as her pot roast with healthy size portions of sides such as mashed potatoes, green beans, and croissants fresh out of the oven. She would sit and visit with us, and laughter filled the evening. She also would make way more than we could eat so that we had plenty of leftovers to get us through the next few days. Also, dinner wasn't complete without a dessert. I would have friends make special requests to her, which usually meant homemade banana pudding.

Years later, when my now adult friends would run into her out and about, they would still ask her when she was cooking again. I'd give anything to sit around that table with family and friends and visit with her just one more time.

She loved to entertain around the table, but she also expected great table manners. I recall as a child she taught my brother and me all the appropriate manners. I asked her one time why it was so important to her, and she told me that she wanted Brian and me to be able to go to dinner with her and Dad, and perhaps business guests or their friends, and be able to use table manners and learn to carry on conversation. She never liked the idea of leaving us at home to go entertain someone. This paid dividends as it taught us a lot at a young age and has been a great life skill that has definitely paid off in building relationships with friends, business clients, and even my own children.

In Mom's last years she became weak with her illness, but even then, it was important for her to host the whole family for gatherings around Christmas, birthdays, Easter, and other occasions. She would make sure everyone had their favorite dish served, and despite how taxing it was, she entertained us all with such grace.

With her passing, the world lost one of the greatest hosts it ever knew, but through the pages of our magazines and the posts on her blog, I have no doubt there are hundreds of thousands of people who were inspired by her and are now paying it forward as they host their family and friends. *—Eric Hoffman*

Eric W. Hoffman

On Seasons, Holidays & Celebrations

Aaron
peace

MAKING OCCASIONS SPECIAL

PHYLLIS LOVED HOLIDAYS, CELEBRATIONS, and family gatherings—and any event involving the grandchildren, Hays and Amelia, was the best. She was a big birthday person. She always wanted to make everyone feel super special on their birthday.

Her favorite holiday was Christmas, especially when we got to be with Hays and Amelia. She always wanted Christmas to be a time when the family was together for a few days. She loved keeping up traditions, often making the Christmas brunch dishes she and her siblings enjoyed growing up. When her sons, Eric and Brian, were young, she loved baking with them and carried on that holiday tradition with the grandkids.

She made so many occasions stand out. When my son, Aaron, graduated from high school, Phyllis wanted to make it special, so the whole family went on a cruise to Alaska. We had a wonderful time with so many great memories. When Aaron graduated from Georgia Tech, we hosted a dinner at Mary Mac's Tea Room in Atlanta for Aaron and his girlfriend, Tory. Our family joined Tory's family for an unforgettable evening. Phyllis loved attending the white coat ceremony for my daughter, Morgan, at Auburn University's veterinary school, and we hosted a celebratory dinner at Acre restaurant following the event.

Watching our kids and grandkids thrive and become their own person brought her great joy. We were huge fans of Amelia's gymnastics meets and Hays's baseball, football, and hunting events. We loved being there for their birthday parties and having them visit each summer for "Camp Gigi."

Being married to Phyllis for 14 years was absolutely the best. She was a master at encouraging those around her and was always there to stand by me through anything. As her health began to fail, I retired from my career to spend every day with her for the time she had left. I will never regret that decision as I will treasure those good days. *—Neal DePiano, husband*

Reworking Vintage Wedding Dresses

We have just finished the wedding anniversary celebrations of the young couples in our family. Every year, I am reminded of the sewing marathon that went on in my home in preparation for those occasions. Oh my, I was so thrilled when my niece, Beth, asked me to make her wedding dress. She wanted a simple dress for a garden wedding. I set about to find antique or vintage lace. While traveling, I happened upon a small shop that was filled with many beautiful things, and hanging in the back were two very old wedding dresses.

I asked the shop owner if I could purchase both dresses, and she gave me the group price of $75! I practically jumped over the counter to pay her, took my treasures, and left. The lace alone was worth so much more to me because it would make my wedding gown creation very special. Beth could choose the one she wanted and then I would save the other gown.

One dress was a very old French lace gown that was barely intact. I knew the lace could be selectively cut, and it would be perfect. But it had to have tender loving care. The other was a couture gown from Bergdorf Goodman with the date 1974 inside.

Beth and I set about to design her dress using the French lace in the godets of the skirt. She preferred the French lace, and it was perfect for the look she wanted.

About the time that we had settled into our plan, my son Eric asked his girlfriend, Katie, to be his bride! Now, we had two weddings, and the festivities were about to begin. Katie loves vintage fashions, and after a lot of subtle hints, I figured out that she wanted the other gown. So, we made our plans to remake and revise the Bergdorf Goodman gown.

Did I mention that Beth and Katie set their wedding dates five days apart? And one bride was in Tennessee, and the other in New York? It was actually so much fun. We mailed photos back and forth and settled on ideas for Katie's dress. Long before the days of texting, this was our only option!

Beth came to our home in Birmingham often for her fittings, and thank goodness, Katie moved to Birmingham several months before the wedding. To add even more fun, my sister, Janice (Beth's mom), was making the bridesmaids' dresses for Beth's wedding. As the weeks progressed and the dresses were all coming together, we pulled in my mom to do the "finger work," as she called hand sewing. I remember the three of us sitting in my sewing room working our hearts out and laughing about this.

The week of the weddings came, and Beth was first. When she came into the garden, I thought I would burst into tears. How could this little girl grow up so fast and now be walking through the garden in her princess dress? She was lovely.

When her wedding was over, we all packed up and went to Louisiana for Katie and Eric's wedding. It was a beautiful day, and I was overwhelmed at thinking that my son was grown up and getting married. We all have experienced these emotions. It is a joyful time in the lives of families.

At each wedding, crazy thoughts kept rolling around in my head. Did I hem the dress straight? Are the ribbons long enough? Did I use the right lace trim? Then, I thought, it's just as it should be. There is nothing more beautiful than a bride on her wedding day. *—June 2016*

Birthday Tradition Makes June Special

June is a rather interesting and exciting month. When I was growing up, June meant no school, sleeping late, and . . . the birthday of a certain someone—a guest writer on this blog, the baby of the family, my sister—Janice!

The day itself didn't really matter. She insisted, and still does, that the entire month is hers. As other people entered the family and children and grandchildren were born, there were other June birthdays that needed to be celebrated. But just as the planets move around the sun, so were our days ordered as we moved around her day, THE day, June 22.

There was only one tiny problem—the willow flies hatched on her birthday at Guntersville Lake. My dad and my mom's brothers always took that week off to

go fishing. So, the birthday festivities always took place in Guntersville, Alabama, with our cousins. Usually, we took a picnic to the lake for Janice's party, where she faithfully reminded us that her birthday was overshadowed by the hatching of the flies and the biting of the bream fish.

Another small problem was that, by this time, school had already been dismissed for the summer break, so Janice missed the requisite birthday cupcakes during class. So, for these reasons, we simply had to proclaim the month of June her birthday month. And hey, why not celebrate for an entire month? Life is passing so quickly that 30 days seems like an appropriate amount of time.

As she has gotten older (not more mature, I might add), Janice is the first one to announce the forthcoming of June. At her party, she takes turns smearing icing on the grandkids' noses, and even my 38-year-old son Brian gets in on it—it's a ritual!

She has a history of running her finger through the icing of any cake Mom made growing up. This tradition began when Mom had made this beautiful cake, iced it pink, and covered the entire top with cherry halves. It was so beautiful. We were all outside playing, and it was time for dinner. When Mom lifted the cake cover to reveal her masterpiece, we discovered Janice had eaten every cherry off the top when no one was looking. The cake had craters that looked like the moon.

The year Janice's second child was born, she was really sweating it out. Could he possibly come on her day and steal the attention? That would never do—no, not at all. He came early in June, thank goodness. He was her first birthday present that year. Then, to complicate her life more, I married Neal who has a June 29 birthday. Oh my gosh, what was I thinking?

Our June month is always fun. This is one of the many reasons why we love Janice—she takes ordinary and makes it special. In this case, that something special turned into tradition. So, June is here and will continue to be Janice's birthday month. Happy birthday to the baby in our family! We love you! *—June 2019*

Hays's Birthday

I love a good birthday celebration. My mom always made birthdays special. She is a good "birthdayer!" As kids, we always got to pick out our favorite dish for supper and our cake!

This past weekend, we celebrated our grandson's 10th birthday. I watched this special young man play baseball and have fun with friends. All grandmothers think this way, but Hays grows so much between visits. Ten years!

I love to look into his eyes when he is telling me what all is going on in his life. He always gives away secrets about his sister's boyfriends. Since she is 8 years old, I haven't started fretting over that yet.

His world is a journey of adventures. We went shopping for a new rod for his upcoming fishing trip, and I watched his eyes sparkle when he gave me details of his fishing lures. We looked at every pole in the sporting goods store, and the ones I liked were not even close to what he needed. I thought they were pretty! He would roll his eyes. "Gigi, you don't buy them because they are pretty!" Who knew?!

The passing of 10 years went too fast for me, so I am grateful that he still loves to spend time with us. I learn so much from him. Ten-year-olds are pretty wise!

Birthdays and the celebrations that go along with them create beautiful memories. I pray each of us will always make those days special for the people in our lives. The extra effort is always worth it. You are never too old to have birthday parties! Just add a cake and candles, and the fun begins! —*June 2018*

Red
cross

"Children make
our lives rich."

Phyllis

Amelia's Art Party

I love sharing party ideas with you because we all are looking for great ideas when planning birthday parties for our little ones—whether grandchildren or children. My daughter-in-law, Katie, planned an art theme this year for Amelia's birthday party. The invitations were adorable and set the tone for a creative afternoon. I loved the presentation and the way she labeled each item with a creative name to echo the party theme.

The mantel in their home was decorated with an array of colorful balloons while a paint can at the end spilled out crepe paper in matching bright colors. One of the cutest ideas was the paintbrushes made from Rice Krispies. Katie took wooden sticks and put them in one side and then dipped the treats in colored chocolates. The paint balls (cake balls) had stems that were inexpensive paintbrushes. And a simple plastic artist palette held the toppings for the cupcake each person created. I am not sure how many decorations got to the top of the cupcake, but it was a delightful time for creative little hands.

Gigi (that's me) got to help make party hats. My mom, known as "Mimi" to the grandkids, found wonderful hats at a dollar store. The children selected silk flowers, bows, and ribbons for their hat, and we used a glue gun to attach them. The wonderful birthday cake featured an artist palette topper, and each layer had brushes, tubes of paint, and art motifs, all made from fondant. Hiding under that was a delicious four-layer white cake.

Katie set up painting stations outside where each child could be creative and paint their own canvas. This was a wonderful idea that brought out the creativity of these kids. These little ones at the party certainly enjoyed being creative and went home covered in paint and icing and wearing party hats. This was a perfect day.
—September 2014

Decoration Day: Honey, You Look Just Like Your Mama

Decoration Day . . . only if you are Southern will you truly get this one. If you are not Southern, it may seem a bit morbid and uncomfortable, but it was truly an expression of respect.

Decoration Day is a Sunday in May or June when your family gathers at the cemetery where all your relatives from generations past (kinfolk) are buried. In the South, most of the time, your deceased family members were all buried in the same cemetery.

This day was important in our family when I was growing up because it was important to my mother and my grandmother and her mother before that. You just didn't miss. It was a command performance. You dressed in your Sunday best, picked flowers from your garden, and carefully strolled through the cemetery, placing blossoms on the graves of your relatives out of respect.

It was not a day we looked forward to because it always occurred on a Sunday in the South that would break sweltering heat records. Hot, hot, hot. And it was a day when hose, heels, and dresses were mandatory—gloves and hats, too, if you had them.

After all, it was your time to shine in front of all the relatives—and you better make your mother proud. On my mother's side of the family, Decoration Day was every Mother's Day. There were seven girl cousins and three boy cousins all decked out. We hugged people we had never seen before and were told a zillion times, "Honey, you look just like your mama." Agreed.

The guys left us, escaping to remove ties, and we seven girls strolled about making our mamas and our grandmother very proud. We would listen to stories of how this was the most important day of the year when they were growing up, as this was when they would see aunts and uncles and long-lost cousins. Afterwards, there was always a huge Sunday lunch back at my grandmother's house, the event for which our mothers had been cooking for a week. You always brought your best dishes and desserts. What a feast!

I know now what my mother had been talking about all those years. The day we dreaded always turned out to be one of the most fun days. It would take us girl cousins all day to tell stories of boys, school, church activities, trips, and projects we were stitching or sewing. We would sit on the big porch swing and talk for hours.

I miss those days of sitting and talking. I wish today our children had that experience of face-to-face conversation. They all have mastered texting and emailing, but nothing replaces the conversations and sharing stories from what soon will be "the good old days."

Decoration Day was about family legacy. It was about showing the respect for your family that transcended generations. The placing of the flowers meant we remembered you and your legacy. Each generation writes their own legacy for others to build on.

And each Decoration Day, we did our mamas proud. *—May 2014*

MOTHER.

Happy Valentine's Day

This week's Valentine's Day celebrations bring to my mind special memories from my teen years.

First, my mom always got a big box of Russell Stover chocolates from my dad. Hers was always the big, bright, shiny red box with a great ribbon or flower on top. Dad got us kids the small version of the red box. It was chocolate heaven! Mom still gets that box every year, and I expect this year will be no different. Some things will never change—nor should they.

When I was a teenager, my mom embroidered a heart-shaped pillow for my sister and one for me. I am sure Keith got something wonderful, but the embroidered pillows were for the girls. Mom saw a photograph of an embroidered pillow in a magazine and sketched her own version on fabric. With her wool embroidery threads, she stitched countless hours on these and finished them with a cream lace border. Her embroidery skills are wonderful, and her creativity is limitless. The entwined garlands of flowers and petite cherub stitched ever so carefully made this pillow stunning. Janice and I have treasured these for years.

As we approach this celebration of the heart, think about a special gift you can make for your loved ones to cherish for years to come. *—February 2016*

Happy Groundhog Day

The whole concept is amazing to me. As one of our most popular and widely anticipated folklore celebrations, Groundhog Day is such a seemingly silly tradition. How does the groundhog seeing its shadow determine if winter remains or if the season has come to an end? I always watch with amazement at the person who holds up the groundhog for all to see. It is a national media sensation.

Apparently, this practice is rooted in a European religious tradition called Candlemas Day. The clergy would bless candles and distribute them to the people. Depending on the weather during Candlemas Day, the people could determine if there would be a "second winter." If the weather was clear and bright, the cold winter fight would continue. If the weather was wet and foul, then they knew the worst of winter had passed.

This same logic applies to the famous groundhog Punxsutawney Phil and his shadow on February 2 each year. If the weather is clear, Punxsutawney Phil will likely see his shadow, and we can plan for another six weeks of winter. If it is overcast and rainy, we can assume spring is right around the corner.

In Pennsylvania this week, there will be a man who picks up the animal and twirls him around for all to see, proclaiming the weather status. I shake my head in disbelief that anyone would want to pick up a groundhog!

Now, let me really share my insight into this situation. It was several months after Neal and I married, and I was standing in the bathroom getting ready to go out to dinner with friends. I looked out the window and staring up at me was this animal. It was big and stood up on its back legs just gazing. I don't know who was more shocked—the animal or me. I called for Neal quickly and explained there was a creature in the backyard that was staring at me. That was a mistake, a big mistake. Neal explained that it was a groundhog and then proceeded to continually harass me about my new and mesmerized admirer.

I watched the groundhog walk off to its burrow, which was located right off the edge of our yard. It comes back into the yard from time to time to eat one of my prized flowers, and it's still big, brown, and very ugly.

Happy Groundhog Day to all of us! *—February 2017*

"Every time I read in the Bible that Mary pondered things in her heart, I am reminded that I do, too! Pondering is not worrying; it is weighing things out in your mind or reflecting on things. I hope you all find beauty in each day. Let's find new ways of making our days better and new ways of celebrating our own worth and individuality."

Phyllis

A Spring Ritual–Easter Dresses

Some of my favorite childhood memories are of the Easter dresses my mother would make for my sister and me. It was the spring ritual that we loved. I have one month to go until Easter when my granddaughter, Amelia, will be wearing her dress made by me, Gigi.

Amelia told me yesterday that she wanted a pink dress again this year. Truthfully, I had planned on white lace, but maybe we can meet in the middle. My grandson, Hays, and I will shop for his outfit, but I have to get started on Amelia's. One month seems like an eternity, but it will pass very quickly.

Every Easter growing up, my sister, Janice, and I were dressed in newly sewn one-of-a-kind dresses and had new shoes to match. You had to choose carefully as these shoes were to last until fall, when new winter shoes would be selected. Mom could sew anything, and she could copy any outfit we loved. One thing was sure: we would have white gloves on as well, which I thought was wonderful because we usually had blue and pink fingers from dyeing eggs the night before.

I don't know about your family, but in the South, Easter was the day to shine! That was the day when little girls wore fancy hats and white, lace-trimmed socks with their Mary Janes. Now, let me say, I was not and still am not a froufrou girl. So, dressing up in hats, gloves, patent leather shoes, and lace-trimmed socks was on the edge for me. But my granddaughter is over the top with froufrou, and the order of the day for her Easter outfit is "more is better." Amelia is a girly girl and wants her skirts "to twirl."

Before the age of children strapped into a car seat, I remember standing up right behind the front seat of the family car going to church on Easter. If we stood, then our skirts were not wrinkled when we arrived. I loved the huge, ruffled petticoat that made your skirt stand out perfectly. It was glorious. We felt so grown up wearing those huge skirts.

We were also versed in the everlasting Southern commandment of fashion: no white shoes before Easter and never after Labor Day. It just wouldn't be right.

Today, I love to sew for my granddaughter, and I take delight in seeing her parade in one of Gigi's creations. Sewing is one of my favorite hobbies, and as long as she will wear my handmade dresses, I will be making them for her like my mother did for me. From the looks of my fabric stash, I will be sewing for decades. What a joy!

—March 2015

Summer Vacation Memories

My family and I have vacationed to many different places over the years. Some of our travels kept us close to home, while others led us farther away to new places. No matter the distance, the most rewarding part of vacations is time spent focused on being together.

As a child, my family traveled all throughout our home state of Alabama. From museums to the beach and everywhere in between, our vacations never had a dull moment. We always loved piling in the car and embarking on another round of summer travels.

One of my favorite vacation memories came during a stop we made for lunch in Prattville, Alabama. We were craving burgers and fries and found ourselves as the only patrons in the restaurant. As you can imagine, we were ravenous after hours spent in the car. My dad was especially hungry. To this day, I'm still convinced that he ordered everything on the menu.

When our order was ready, rather than simply saying "order up," our waitress proceeded to yell out each individual item on our order. I can still hear her Southern drawl as she recited, "Two double cheeseburgers, three strawberry milkshakes (hold the cherry on one!), a large onion ring, a kid's chicken finger plate . . ." By the time Dad made it to the counter to claim our food, she had almost reached the end of our lengthy order. As the last item was called out, my mother got her signature twinkle in her eye and, in her best singsong voice, ended the list with, "And a partridge in a pear tree!" Everyone burst into hysterical laughter, and Dad was totally embarrassed. It was a signature move of my mom's.

The reason that moment is so precious to me is that we didn't have to travel around the world to find it. We were simply a few hours from home, eating burgers as a family. All it took was Mom's seamless incorporation of a favorite Christmas song to make that lunch unforgettable.

I hope that no matter where your travels take you this summer, you are surrounded by those you love, enjoying small moments together. May your summer days be full of laughter . . . and lots of burgers and fries! —*July 2016*

Fall and My Favorite Things

This time of year is so revitalizing for me, and I just can't help but soak up all of the wonderful things that autumn has to offer! It's difficult to narrow it down, but some of my favorite things about fall include football, spiced pumpkin lattes, pumpkin pies, and white pumpkins. Yes, white pumpkins. They are all the rage in decorating. I have one question. When did these things appear? Growing up, I never saw a white pumpkin . . . every pumpkin I ever saw was orange. Yes, that's it, orange.

Charlie Brown movies are my favorites, especially *It's the Great Pumpkin, Charlie Brown*. I still watch that movie every Halloween and relive a bit of my childhood. It's about orange pumpkins. ORANGE.

Orange is totally out of style, I guess, giving way to white, green, and turquoise. These specimens with natural white skin are bred by pumpkin growers, and decorating with them is so refreshing. I love to use them in arrangements with bittersweet. What a great combination!

Another fall treat at the top of my list is the Pumpkin Spice Latte. I think it's safe to call the PSL a cultural phenomenon. As I thought about picking up a steamy cup of my own the other day, I couldn't help but wonder how in the world a latte built such a loyal fan base. But I've come to realize it's more about what it represents than the drink itself. Taking a sip is a luxury that can only be experienced at a certain time of year. If we could have a PSL in February, it would just make the whole experience rather lackluster.

It's a good thing that pumpkin pie is near and dear to my heart because the flavor is everywhere. Take one trip to the grocery store this time of year, and you'll see what I mean: pumpkin pie–flavored popcorn, cereal, oatmeal, and even body lotion! I'm a huge advocate for all things pumpkin flavored, but my true affection is for the delicious, classic pumpkin pie. It's the dessert that started it all. In all the craze over the years, some might forget the delicacy of a simple buttery piecrust with a

sweet, creamy, and perfectly spiced custardy filling. But not me; this dish will always make its way onto my table during autumn.

Lastly, nothing says fall like football. My love for weekends full of football in the South runs deeper than the game itself. I love that football is something that brings people together. Think about it—we plan, pack, cook, bake, drive, set up tents, and all the in-between to spend game day surrounded by friends and family cheering on our teams. And whether those cheers are for the same team or not, there is still a sense of community and togetherness there.

These things and more are why I love this season. Oh, and did I mention the relief from summer's heat that finally comes in autumn's months? Get outside and enjoy the beauty of fall's colors and crisp air! It's rejuvenating! *—September 2018*

It's Almost Kickoff Time!

I just got an email that my football tickets have shipped for the forthcoming college football season. I can hardly believe it's time to pull out the tailgating recipes and start planning. I look forward to this time of year with great anticipation, but football season also brings back many memories.

When my siblings and I were kids, Mom and Dad would take us to Friday night high school football games, and if Dad had tickets to the University of Alabama game, we'd go again on Saturday. I asked him why he took us to the games, and he said with a smile, "It was cheaper than a babysitter." Great answer!

When my sons, Eric and Brian, were in high school and homecoming time rolled around, I would reflect on the good old days when I was in high school and ask them what kind of corsages we needed to order for their dates. Much to my amazement, corsages today include everything from roses to orchids to carnations. So, I must ask the obvious question: whatever happened to the football mum? Yes, the mum—the one with your school letters made of pipe cleaners and inserted into the center of the flower.

I remember the first time I saw one of those beauties was on my mom. Dad had taken us to the University's homecoming in Tuscaloosa, Alabama, and she wore a cream mum with crimson and white ribbon streamers. It was carefully pinned on her glorious, tailored suit. The whole look was stunning! We dressed up for the games, back then. I am talking suit, heels, pantyhose, and matching purse, even though the temperatures soared into the 90s.

When I got to high school and homecoming was fast approaching, I was secretly hoping for one of the mums from my date. At that time, the competition was to see who could sport the longest ribbons hanging from the corsage.

A year or so later, my sister, Janice, made the cheerleading squad, and for homecoming that year, she didn't have a date as she was concentrating on the cheerleading events surrounding the whole weekend. My brother, Keith, and I were determined she was going to have the traditional mum and ordered one for her with the requisite pipe-cleaner lettering, plus we ordered 36-inch-long ribbon streamers that were sure to hang to the hem of her cheerleading uniform. Done.

That particular evening, when the cheerleaders came out, there Janice was with the longest streamers. Mission accomplished. Those are the dream nights that live forever.
—August 2014

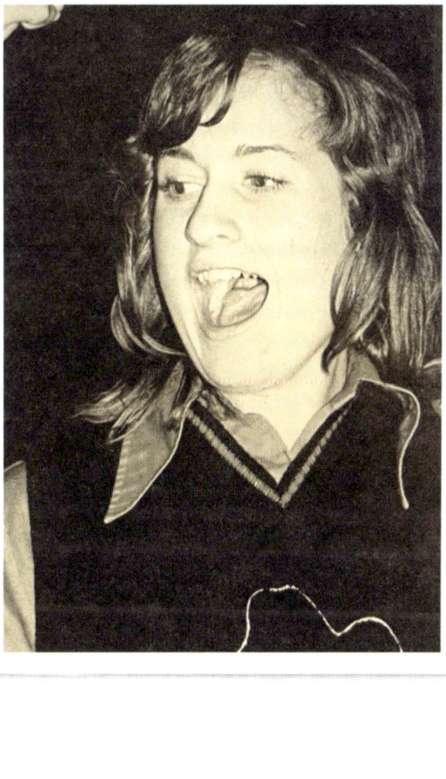

WRIGLEYS
DOUBLEMINT
CHEWING GUM
WRIGLEYS
DOUBLEMINT

Bring the Perfect Halloween Costume to Life

In the South, the month of September provides our last glimpse of summer and first look toward fall. One of my favorite parts of fall is Halloween with its candy and creative costumes!

My fondest Halloween memory was when my twins, Eric and Brian, were only 3 years old. One of the best parts about having twins is being able to play off the twin theme and dress them alike. I was inspired by the Wrigley's Doublemint gum slogan: "Double Your Pleasure, Double Your Fun," which I think is perfect for twins. I made their Doublemint gum costumes, and the boys looked so cute. They even won the costume contest at our church's fall festival!

The Doublemint costumes lived on in infamy and set the bar for every costume of theirs from that day forward. In 2013, unbeknownst to me, the boys decided that the costumes would make a triumphant return for the annual Hoffman Media costume contest. On the day of the contest, Eric and Brian showed up at work in brand-new versions of the Doublemint costumes! They had enlisted my sister, Janice, to recreate the costumes. I absolutely loved seeing these cherished childhood costumes brought to life again. Much to their chagrin, Eric and Brian did not win the office's costume contest. However, they absolutely made my day, and it was wonderful to see how much that costume still meant to us almost 30 years after its original debut.
—October 2016

Thanksgiving & Gratitude

Gratitude. To each of us, that word has different meanings. What we are thankful for differs as well. And as we age, I think it takes on new meanings with the passing of time. What used to be the traditional large family gathering on Thanksgiving Day—women in the kitchen, men by the TV watching football rivalries, and kids playing outside until the dinner is ready—has changed or is not always possible.

Enter Friendsgiving. I heard this term several weeks ago, and I was intrigued by it. That is a wonderful idea. Why not have a gathering of friends who mean so much? A gathering of friends takes the place of the traditional family when one is alone or can't physically be with their family for whatever reason.

The love of friends should be celebrated, whether on Thanksgiving Day or during this holiday season. Take this time to get together and tell why you are thankful for each friend.

It would take me days to tell all the wonderful things for which I am thankful. This past year has been a mixture of challenges, illness, death of loved ones, happy times with grandchildren, and many moments of joy! Through it all, we had friends that walked with us. Neal and I are very blessed, and we really have a deeper love for family and friends who have walked with us.

During this time, writing notes of gratitude would mean so much to the people in your life. Simple words change lives. Words encourage and give hope.

Practicing gratitude in our daily lives is one of the best ways to create a joyful existence. Think about it. When you're feeling appreciative of the people, places, and things in your life, there is a great sense of contentment and little room for negativity.

Here are 10 ways we can practice gratitude daily and, in turn, live a more positive and inspiring life:

1. Give one sincere compliment daily.

2. Try to give up complaining for one week. Each time something bothers you, try to think about something positive. (This is easier said than done, I know, but it's a great way to start.)

3. Get involved in a cause that's important to you. Whether you donate time, money, or talent, your contribution will be greatly appreciated.

4. Keep a gratitude journal where you record three things that you are grateful for each day. If you have the time, try to do this once in the morning and once before bed.

5. There's a Thanksgiving Day tradition where, after saying grace, those seated around the table share something they are thankful for. Why not practice this year-round?

6. Say "thank you." This is not groundbreaking, and most of us do it anyway, but remember to thank loved ones, even for the mundane things that we might normally take for granted.

7. Write a letter of gratitude. Thank-you notes are not only for receiving gifts! Take time and write someone who has made a profound impact on your life. It will bring joy to you both.

8. Look at mistakes as opportunities for growth. We all make mistakes, and when we look back, we usually learn something from them, too!

9. Smile.

10. Spend quality time with those you love. Whether cooking, crafting, or taking a walk, make time to really connect with family and friends. —*November 2021*

Small Gifts with Big Impacts

I was sitting in the waiting room at my doctor's office, and a lady came over and handed me a little white crocheted angel. She said, "I wanted to make sure you received one of my angels." I took the delicate ornament in my hand and looked around the room at other patients admiring her work. She returned to her seat where she proceeded to make more angels.

I pondered this wonderful act of kindness to all of us who were in the waiting room. Most people there knew that room all too well and were awaiting their turn for chemotherapy. I was there for my biweekly anemia test and have observed many acts of love and encouragement during my time there.

I don't know the woman's name who was crocheting, but all I could think of was how she used her gifts to bless others. I don't know if she was a patient or was there with a patient, but she glowed with joy as she plied every stitch. Each seat had an angel placed on it with a little tag that read, "Made with love . . . just for you." I now call this precious woman the Stitching Angel and wish her all the happiness that she has brought to those lucky enough to receive her angels. Thank you, Stitching Angel!

I will treasure this lovely token and hang it on my tree. It will serve as a reminder to me during the Christmas season that sharing love and encouragement with others should be my goal this season and every season. *—November 2018*

My Near Failed Effort to Make Mom's Christmas Cookies

As children, my siblings, Janice and Keith, and I awaited with wonder the lovely gifts, mouthwatering food, and glad-hearted bustle surrounding Christmas. We relished the abundance of homemade treats at this time of year. Mom always had Cookie Day when we were growing up. It was a whole day dedicated to making her sugar cookies and icing them! Her recipe for these classic Christmas cookies had to be made a day ahead so that the dough could be refrigerated before we rolled it out for cutting.

Fast-forward many years when we were publishing the first anniversary issue of *Southern Lady* magazine. We decided that we would photograph snowflake-shaped cookies to feature on the cover. I volunteered to make Mom's recipe and share it with our readers. That evening, I went by Mom's to get the recipe. She went to her cupboard where the cookie cutters were kept. She took down the box and tore off the lid where the recipe was printed; she just laughed and said this was her family recipe!

I left and went by the store on my way home to get the ingredients. I carried the recipe in and shopped diligently, collecting everything I needed. It was dark when I came out, and I went home to mix up the dough so it could chill overnight.

I set out all the ingredients and was all ready to start when I realized I had lost the recipe. I dumped out the contents of my purse—nothing. I called the manager of the grocery store and explained this was an emergency as I must have dropped the recipe as I was shopping. He said he would call back after he walked around the store.

When he called, he said he was so sorry, but he had found no recipe. My heart sank. I did what any self-respecting desperate woman would do: I got in my car to return to the store and drove to the parking lot where I must have dropped the recipe—nothing. Since it was dark, I decided to get out of my car and walk around the area where I had parked. About that time, bright headlights were shining on me. I stopped dead in my tracks. I could hear the laughter coming from the car. It was the minister of music from our church and his entire family. I forgot to mention that I had on my pink fuzzy robe and fuzzy slippers. I just thought I could pull this off with no one seeing me, but I was wrong.

Not only had I embarrassed myself, but I lost the recipe. I returned home, and while I was driving, all I could think of was the fact that I had single-handedly lost the family recipe. What would I do? I couldn't tell Mom. So, I called my sister, Janice, and told her of my dilemma. She laughed and told me she had written down the recipe several years ago, and she read it to me.

The magazine photo shoot came off without a hitch, and the recipe was saved. Holiday baking is and always will be very important in our family.

Now, I'm excited to share the recipe for Mimi's Cookies. I hope it brings some extra cheer to your holidays this year. *—December 2015*

MIMI'S COOKIES

Makes about 72 cookies

½ cup unsalted butter, softened
1 cup granulated sugar
2 large eggs
½ teaspoon vanilla extract
4 cups all-purpose flour
2 teaspoons baking powder
1 teaspoon kosher salt
2 to 3 tablespoons whole milk or heavy whipping cream
Food coloring (optional)
Icing (recipe follows)
Sprinkles (optional)

1. In the bowl of a stand mixer fitted with the paddle attachment, beat butter and sugar at medium speed until fluffy, 3 to 4 minutes, stopping to scrape sides of bowl. Add eggs, one at a time, beating well after each addition. Beat in vanilla.
2. In a large bowl, whisk together flour, baking powder, and salt. With mixer on low speed, gradually add flour mixture to butter mixture, beating until combined. Add 2 tablespoons milk or cream, beating until a moist, thick dough forms. Add remaining 1 tablespoon milk or cream, if necessary. (Dough should not be crumbly.) Beat in food coloring, if desired. (For multiple colors of dough, divide dough into batches and add desired amount of food coloring.) Cover and refrigerate for at least 2 hours.
3. Preheat oven to 375°.
4. On a lightly floured surface, roll dough to ¼-inch thickness. Using desired cutters, cut dough, and place on ungreased baking sheets.
5. Bake until golden, about 12 minutes. Let cool completely. Frost cookies with Icing, adding sprinkles, if desired.

ICING

Makes about ½ cup

1½ cups confectioners' sugar
1 large egg white
1 teaspoon vanilla extract
Food coloring (optional)

1. In the bowl of a stand mixer fitted with the paddle attachment, beat confectioners' sugar, egg white, vanilla, and food coloring, if desired, at medium speed until smooth. Icing should dry quickly after frosting cookies and be hard to the touch.

Christmas Is Almost Here!

I love watching children at Christmas. I adore the sticky faces and fingers of a zealous candy cane eater and the colored icing that always manages to appear on each child's outfit during cookie decorating. I love all the fun holiday get-togethers at this time of year. One of the season's highlights for us as children was Christmas tree shopping.

Scattered throughout our city, there are various Boy Scout groups that host Christmas tree lots stocked with wonderful evergreens. It was always a cold night when all of us would bundle up and head to our favorite tree sale. I can still remember the fragrance as we walked down every row. There is nothing like fresh evergreens.

We could never agree on a tree. The kids wanted the tallest tree on the lot, with total disregard for our home's ceiling height! But our mom and dad would always find the perfect one to fit in our home. The Boy Scouts would nail the tree into the stand, and we would take our prized possession home.

When it was all said and done, our tree stood tall and was always interesting. Dad would get out the lights and place them on the tree first. Back then, we had those big lights that got hot on the tree, not the tiny cool lights of today. Then came the ornaments we had collected or made through the years. We had some that were so pitiful. They always garnered a laugh, but we hung them anyway. Others were very beautiful ones that Mom had painted.

After all the ornaments were on, it was time for the finishing touch—the icicles! Most kids today just don't know about this ritual. At our house, the aluminum strands had to be hung one at a time to make sure they were perfectly straight. It started out that way, but by the time we finished, my brother was throwing the tinsel by the handful just to get it done. We always had carols playing on the stereo while this was going on, and the music just made the season. We each had a favorite, and we would all sing along from time to time. After about a week, every time you walked through the room, you would hear the dry needles falling from the tree branches and hitting the floor. It was a Charlie Brown tree by Christmas Day!

Stockings were fun, and we loved the small things we got in them every Christmas morning. Christmas memories are priceless. We found out just a few years ago that my brother would talk my mom into letting him open his presents early and then rewrap them days before Christmas . . . he never could fake a surprise! But it was a tradition they shared between the two of them. Our church choir always had a marvelous cantata that was presented the week before Christmas. Our family was always the first one there to get a good seat. Dad held down the tenor section. Mom usually was involved in the stage sets or costumes.

Christmas for us was, is, and always will be about family. This year, all of us will be home for Christmas. All the grandchildren, great-grandchildren, and my siblings and their significant others will be at our home for our family Christmas brunch. Mom and Dad will be surrounded by their family to have all the fun you could pack into one day. Dad will give us all a chocolate Santa Claus, and Mom will make her famous angel biscuits. How blessed we are to have each other!

Celebrating the birth of Christ is a sacred time for us. I hope, this year, you will find Christ at the center of your holiday. May you be filled with joy, love, and peace for this blessed time of year. *—December 2017*

"To: Mom, From: Santa"

As I child, I refused to believe there was no Santa! I am the oldest of three children, so I was the first to go to school and hear all the opinions on this subject. One weirdo kid proceeded to tell me that it was not true and that my parents were fibbing. But they would never, right? Either way, it worked for me! I loved Santa, and I still do today. The magic and make-believe are just a part of my childhood.

Then one Christmas Eve, the truth was revealed by accident, quite literally. We all were sent to bed, and the strain of lying still when you were wide awake was horrible.

As I was lying there, I heard a noise from the basement below. Now, knowing Santa was on the move that evening, I wasn't very disturbed. However, I began listening closer to the thumping and bumping up the basement stairs. It was a sound that I recognized and a laughter that was all too familiar.

The next morning, under the tree sat my beautiful suitcase and train case that just so happened to be on my list. Long story short, the thumping was Mom falling up the stairs with the luggage and getting tickled at herself. I looked at her with a sheepish grin, and after my siblings had left the room, I asked, "Fall up the stairs?" She just burst into laughter as only she can. I knew, but it didn't matter. It was all just so much fun! Did it destroy my belief in the unseen? Not for a second! I wasn't about to miss out on keeping up the charade for my siblings.

When my twin sons were young, they would test Santa and ask him to bring things that were not on their list. One year, they told me on Christmas Eve that they asked Santa to bring ME something special. My heart sank as they explained that they were testing Santa to see if he was real! After prying, I discovered that they had asked him for coral-colored shoes for me, since they knew I adored that color. Being the dead of winter, that color would be nowhere to be found in any store. It was a pretty crafty plan for two children!

What they didn't know was that I had purchased a pair of coral pumps a few months earlier when the summer shoes were on sale, and they were tucked away in my closet. So, I wrapped them and slipped them under the tree. The next morning, two blue-eyed little fellows were certain they had solved the mystery. The presents were opened, and there was only one gift left. The tag read, "To: Mom, From: Santa."

Their little mouths dropped. They brought the box to me and stood right over me while I opened it. They giggled and blushed—shocked that Santa had granted their wish! I was just relieved I had bought those shoes, and the fun would go on another year. See, I knew good things come from shopping sales!

I look back on those days with great fondness, both my childhood and time with my boys. The magic of Christmas abounds when there are children around. I hope you experience the joy of children this year. Merry Christmas to you and yours!
—December 2018

Jingle Bells

I love Christmas ornaments, and I have so many. Among my favorites are those that my grandchildren have made for me—each so special. Others are for themed trees like one I did years ago with a music motif or my hand-painted blue-and-white collection. Every year as I unpack them, I let my mind think back to wonderful times and beautiful celebrations of Christmas.

When Neal and I got married, we started a silver jingle bell ornament collection. Since we were married on December 23, these bells are a treasured Christmas keepsake. The night we married, we gave each of our kids and grandchildren a silver snowflake to remember our special night as a family. Every year, we add another bell to our tree to commemorate our anniversary.

This year, I gave two newlywed couples a silver bell engraved with the date to hang on their tree for their first Christmas together—something you may want to consider starting for a new grandchild or new member of your family. If you paint or sew, you could also make dated ornaments for them.

I love passing down ornaments, too! My son Brian has two of my Grandmother Norton's ornaments that hung on her tree when I was a little girl. They are faded and exude years of love packing and unpacking them. I was so happy he wanted them, and he will be the fourth generation to hang them on the tree every year.

I could write forever about ornaments, as they usually tell stories of special times in our lives. During this beautiful season, I wish you love and joy. You are special to me, and as we celebrate this season together, know you are treasured. *—December 2017*

The Most Controversial Holiday Dessert: Fruitcake

OK, let's talk about the one thing that gets everyone in a tizzy during the holidays—fruitcake! Just the mention of it makes some people crazy, and others hear it and can't wait! I just wonder how many recipes are out there for this steadfast treat.

My most favorite fruitcake of all is an Icebox Fruitcake my Grandmother Norton made every year. And believe it or not, it was a no-bake recipe! My family could eat an entire loaf in no time flat! I have her handwritten recipe, and I just love the haphazard listing of ingredients: "a batch of pecans, a jar of cherries, graham crackers," and many other unmeasured ingredients. I adore reading it!

The truth is, only she knew how many pecans were in "a batch," and she bought only one size jar of cherries. Her intuition in the kitchen was incredible—just a quick stir and a few hours of chilling and out came her masterpiece and beloved family favorite!

Now, I am on a mission to make my own version of this cherished delicacy. I am going to bake a fruitcake with only the fruits I like. Because if you only put in fruits you like, then you should like the cake! Simple logic, right? My plan is to start with a basic spice cake and add in nuts and fruits from there. This should be interesting. *—November 2018*

The Christmas Story Renews Us Each Year

I have read the Christmas story many times over the years, and each time, God reveals something new. Throughout the Bible, there are two references to Mary pondering something in her heart.

I imagine she was in quite a quandary over the news that she was expecting. When our "normal" is interrupted, whether good or bad, that causes us to ponder deeply our circumstances. What does ponder mean? I always think of sleepless nights—tossing and turning—trying to solve problems in my mind. I flip pillows, switch from side to side, check the clock, and sometimes get up and go to my favorite chair. Well, maybe, this is considered fretting.

Pondering is a profound consideration of things that are deep in our souls. It is an analysis of all the facts and how it affects us personally. In Mary's situation, she was carrying the Savior. How do you begin to ponder that? To be chosen for this royal appointment is an enormous calling, and yet, in her time, it was met with great concern. What will people think? How will Joseph react? Will I become an outcast or be removed from my family?

This is often how we approach surprising circumstances in our lives. When things happen unexpectedly, our default might be creating a laundry list of worries. But let's ponder this instead: there is a divine plan for our lives, and that truth never changes, even when circumstances do.

The little baby that broke the silence in the night changed everything. And he still does today. I love Christmas Eve because it makes me stop and reflect on the life-changing event that occurred thousands of years ago in a humble stable to a young girl who was chosen by God. It changed my life, and for this, I celebrate the beautiful season of Christmas with great gratitude. Merry Christmas, dear friends!

—December 2014

"Are we carving out time for things we really want to do— things that will lead us to the place we have dreamed of being? Today, spend some time reflecting on that thought."

Phyllis

New Year, New Start

Happy New Year to all of you! I hope 2018 is a glorious year for each of you. I have already made my list of things I want to do during this next year. I am not going to call the list my resolutions, but merely things that need my attention. That sounds better to me.

I think if I could sum up the number one thing that has come to my mind, it would be this: let go of the past. I didn't get all the tasks done that I wanted to do during the holidays. I have thought many times that I simply waited too late to get started. We had a wonderful Christmas, but as I usually do, I have gone down the list in my mind of the things I intended to do and didn't complete.

Letting go means wiping the slate clean. Holding on to things that should have been or could have been is like an anchor—not only in the busyness of the holidays but in everyday life. I saw the greatest post on Pinterest the other day that really caught my attention: "Never be a prisoner of your past. It was a lesson, not a life sentence."

Now, that will make you stop and think. We have to let go of things we deemed failures or did not accomplish. It can be different for each person. This year, I've already learned that I need to start preparing earlier for things that matter.

What about you? Are you ready to make 2018 a great year? Let's get started together by acknowledging that we failed at some things that are in our past and move on. We will walk together this year and have a great time. *—January 2018*

Happy New Year Again

Last time, I wrote about things I wanted to accomplish in the new year, and I am sure your list is full, too. I do want to share a story with you, as this morning I did something that I have been wanting to do for years.

First, let me give you the backstory. When I was in the fifth grade, we started cursive writing with a fountain pen. We had graduated from pencil to pen, and this was a dream come true. There were no felt-tips or rollerballs like there are today, just ballpoint pens. So, getting a fountain pen was heaven.

My first pen was a typical school pen. You inserted cartridges and wrote away. My ink was navy blue or black. I loved the sound of the pen moving across the paper and seeing the flow of ink. I always managed to get the ink all over my fingers as I changed the cartridges.

One day, a sweet friend of mine walked in with her second fountain pen (not in the budget for me) and proceeded to write in peacock blue ink. I went weak and could hardly think. Peacock blue ink! She had just achieved a status untouched by the rest of us. I watched with intense jealousy as she wrote her notes with this glorious ink.

Years later, I was shopping one day at a store that was having a moving sale. The closeout table contained items the owner had found in the back storage room. There it was! A box with a glass bottle of peacock blue ink—I grabbed it quickly and just rejoiced at this find. My racing heart slowed down after I had paid for the ink. I took it home and tucked it away with my prized possessions. I never opened it. I just looked at it from time to time and thought of the day my friend premiered it.

Today, I decided 2022 is the year of doing things I have put off, and using this ink is at the top of the list. I went to the hiding place and carefully retrieved this 35-year-old bottle of ink.

I got my fountain pen and drew up the ink into the cartridge and wrote my first card. The ink was perfect, as if it were brand-new. Through this blog, you know of my love of fountain pens and colorful inks. I love all of them. But today was special. The old vintage ink had come to life and brought such joy as I wrote. My handwriting was even neater as each letter was formed. I do have a little ink stain on my fingers . . . why not?

Let's make 2022 a year of doing things we have placed on the back burner. It doesn't have to be anything big, just something that will delight you. When the ink is gone, I will smile and remember this pleasure. —*January 2022*

A GENEROUS SPIRIT

MY MOTHER-IN-LAW, Phyllis Hoffman DePiano, was by far the most brilliant and talented person I have ever encountered. I can think of almost nothing that she couldn't do. She was a concert pianist and organist, an heirloom seamstress, a painter, a wonderful cook, and a consummate hostess.

Phyllis had a great sense of style and was always perfectly dressed. She had a penchant for red nails, and she had an amazing shoe collection. I was only so lucky to wear the same size! I will never forget her buying us matching red patent leather pumps at a store on Fifth Avenue in New York City. I often joked that God held the saltshaker of gifts and talents over Phyllis's head a bit longer than the rest of us. She was all these things and much more, but her greatest gift, in my opinion, was her generous spirit. She shared all that she had and all that she was with everyone around her.

When I got engaged, she asked me what kind of wedding dress I thought I wanted. I told her, and she said matter-of-factly, "Well, I can do that!" You can't imagine my surprise and fear, quite honestly. I hadn't known her long enough to know just how capable she was. The wedding dress she made for me was beautiful, and I hope, one day, my daughter, Amelia, might wear it. Phyllis made Amelia and me clothes for years. My favorite Mardi Gras ball gown is a magenta velvet one-shoulder Phyllis wonder. I cherish it and will always look back fondly on the memory of shopping with her at Promenade in New Orleans for the beautiful fabric imported from Spain.

She was never too busy for my children, even with all she had going on. She'd talk to my son, Hays, on the phone for hours . . . literally. She also never missed a chance to take Amelia and me to have tea at The Windsor Court or to go on shopping sprees. She did "Camp GiGi" in the summer for Amelia and her friends, teaching them some of the skills she had honed over the years. We all miss Phyllis, but her spirit lives on through the children. I just know Phyllis is up there in heaven playing the organ with bright red paint on her nails and those red patent leather shoes on her feet. —*Katie Hoffman, daughter-in-law*

On Following Life's Passions

A JOURNAL IN HER HEART

PHOTO COURTESY OF PHILLIP DUPREE.

WHEN I WAS 17 YEARS OLD and my missionary parents were returning to their overseas assignment, Phyllis and her family took me under their wings in the fall of 1984. I spent many weekends with the Hoffmans and even lived with them off and on through college and after, until I married. At some point along the way, Phyllis became my "adopted" mom. Consequently, I was well aware that she was a collector—mostly of fine fabrics, buttons (old and new), and needlework implements but also of Princess Diana memorabilia, tea wares, blue-and-white china, and other "treasures." These items were tucked away in various antique and built-in cabinets, but some were prominently displayed in other parts of her home.

When Phyllis and her second husband, Neal DePiano, were preparing to move from the large house she had built and occupied for more than two decades, I offered to help her pack the items she deemed too precious to let the movers box up. We first tackled her collections of blue-and-white dishes, porcelain teapots, and rolling pins, among others. As we pulled things out of kitchen and dining room drawers and cabinets, Phyllis could easily recall who gave her what and when—such as the silver tea strainer and stand I had given her in 2003 when she turned 50—or where she had purchased something herself. I now wish we had taken the time then to record the provenance of each item, but, alas, we had a firm deadline to be ready for the movers.

As we shifted our focus to the sewing room, I thought I knew what was in store, but I was still surprised by all the stash that was squirreled away in the antique sewing table and built-ins. I was amazed at how Phyllis remembered where she had obtained each bolt of fabric or piece of antique lace and for what project. A scrap of either would bring to mind a garment and the person for whom she had made it. She even had the beads she used when she reworked the gown and veil from her late-1970s first marriage for me to wear for my 1992 wedding. Phyllis identified thimbles that had belonged to her Grandmother Norton, ones that had been given to her by other people, and still others that she had procured. There was a funny story, a moving memory, or a real purpose attached to almost everything we pulled out, which made culling any of it a challenge and packing a slow process. As we worked to fill each box, it was beautiful to hear the remembrances associated with the people whose love or friendship made keeping those items a must. It was clear to me that she had been keeping a lifelong journal in her heart. —*Lorna Reeves, friend and* TeaTime *editor*

The Charm and Personality of Well-Curated Collections

I often find myself inspired by the home décor captured in our magazines. Peering into a person's home tells a special kind of story. The color palette, the fabrics and furnishings, and especially the collections are a clue into what the homeowners love, where they've been, and what sets them at ease.

I'm especially impressed by the way well-curated collections lend personality and interest to a space. A mix of something like antique scissors and collectible thimbles, for instance, reveals a beloved hobby. Even the quirky souvenirs from a tourist shop make a fun little statement as well as reveal the places someone has traveled. At the same time, those elements soften a space and make it unique.

I recently had the privilege of speaking at Bromberg's, a local jewelry and giftware store, for a Vietri holiday event. As the women and men came in and took their places, I asked, "How many of you collect china or dishes?" Every hand went up in the room. Now, why should I be surprised? You're familiar with my love for blue-and-white china. You know I love beautiful tableware and have always loved seeing the new items that are introduced ever year. But I should have realized I am one among many who collect!

Finding a new piece for your collection is always exciting. Exploring antiques stores and vintage shops for that perfect item can even be exhilarating. Even if I don't purchase it, I love keeping an eye out for the special things I feel connected to. There's a thrill in the hunt for a collector.

If you don't have a collection, think about what you might enjoy. It just takes one piece to get started. *—November 2018*

MIMI D' AMOUR

A Passion for Blue and White

I have a passion for blue and white, a classic color combination that adds excitement to any room. Anyone who has ever shared a meal at my home will tell you that my enthusiasm extends to blue-and-white china.

When my Grandmother Norton introduced me to the Blue Willow pattern, my love affair with blue-and-white china blossomed. She had a beautiful Blue Willow oval vegetable dish that was present at every meal when I was growing up; she always served her prized peas and beans in it.

I was the lucky one in the family to inherit her treasured bowl, and today, it is displayed in my kitchen where I love seeing the tiny cracks that indicate it was worn from serving endless food to our family. The bowl represents happy times around the table. It was the first blue-and-white piece I owned, and it inspired me to start my own collection. I haven't stopped collecting since.

Many men and women around the world share my passion. One of my favorite patterns is Blue Calico by Staffordshire. I was in college when I found this delightful pattern at a local antiques store. Although the pieces were new, imported from England, I knew I had to have them. The proprietor was kind enough to allow me to make installment payments until I had paid for eight place settings. I was the happiest girl in the world when I brought my treasures home.

I am still thrilled to set my table with the Blue Calico dinnerware. I have several other blue-and-white patterns in my cabinet (which shocks no one who loves blue and white), and I use them individually or combined. I mix in antique patterns as well.

If you are thinking about collecting blue-and-white dishware, consider starting with a beautiful old platter. Find one that you dearly love and display it on an easel or use it as a serving piece. Little by little, you will find wonderful pieces to add to your collection. Then before long, your china cabinet will be overflowing, and you will have a handsome collection. *—March 2014*

Cherished Tokens

It's funny what cherished tokens we accumulate during our lifetime. I have very special notes from my sons and grandchildren, including hand-drawn portraits of me and notes written in their beginner handwriting. When one of them discovers my treasures, they always say, "I can't believe you kept this!" Are you kidding? Those are priceless little tokens that mean you were thought of in a special way.

I still have one card from my grandmother, who wrote inside, "How proud I am of you," and that just makes my day. I keep it in a little chest on my desk. We all like to be remembered. I have sticky notes from my kids and pictures in their finest Crayola coloring work and pressed flowers from special moments. These remind me of my blessings and the special moments when they shared cherished tokens with me.

Why don't we do that more as adults? I think of it and then something distracts me. How fun it would be to send a sticky note to a friend or family member that says, "Thinking of you!" Or perhaps put a piece of ribbon in an envelope and mail it to be used as a bookmark. It's the little tokens that touch our hearts. I plan on doing a better job of sharing tokens of love, and I hope that, in years to come, they will mean something to the recipient. *—February 2021*

Chocolate Dessert
Base: 2 cups flour
2 sticks butter
1 c. chopped pecans
Bake at 325°-
20-30 min.
Cool
Top:
6 oz. choc. chips (semi-sweet)
1 tsp vanilla
1-3 tbs. sugar
1 egg
1 tbs. instant coffee
3/4 cup hot milk
Blender - 1 minute
Angel Biscuits
1 package dry yeast
½ cup lukewarm water
3/4 cup shortening
5 cups self-rising flour
2 cups buttermilk
1 Teaspoon soda
3 Tablespoons sugar
Rocky Road Ice Cream
what's cookin'
Recipe from the kitchen of

The One that Got Away

You know, we Southern women love to brag about our gardens. It is almost as exciting as bragging about our secret recipe for the pound cake everyone raves about at supper club. When I was growing up, at right about this time of the year, my mama's perennial garden was in full bloom. Today, it is again, and we take great delight in swapping stories about what "came back" from the prior year.

I plant new things each year to add to the mix of favorites. The joke at our house is "Oh, no! She has bought more bulbs." Yes, that's right. I am totally consumed with catalogues and websites that offer collections of bulbs and plants. Not only that, but I can actually visualize exactly where they need to be planted to create the picturesque garden that will bloom every year.

Several years ago, right after Neal and I married, Aaron announced that he wanted to have prom dinner at our home, complete with a prom photo session around the fountain. Neal was thrilled that his son wanted to host the dinner for 12 couples at the ranch, and I set in with the master plan of creating the garden "look" for the photographic background. I figured out the time it would take for a tulip bulb to bloom from planting to blossom.

On the appointed day, I was out there in the cold with my flats of pansies and bags and bags of tulip bulbs. I had the plan, and I was in motion. Coupled with the already planted 'Knock Out' roses and lamb's ears, these new additions would result in a garden that would be life-changing. Did I mention that all the parents were to come with their children for the photo session? So, I was making plans for a garden moment that would be viewed by more than 75 people at sunset on that magical night, a crowning accomplishment.

As the weeks progressed and the little shoots started emerging, I was right on schedule. My timing was perfect. The week of prom had finally arrived. The menu was exactly what Aaron wanted, and all that was left was to spiff up the garden. The tulips could not have been more beautiful poking their heads through the mounds of pansies.

Three days before prom, I woke up ready to take my usual early morning stroll through the masterpiece garden with my cup of coffee. I opened the door to find everything in my garden was gone. Gone. Not a bloom in sight. I think my face went numb, and I couldn't utter a word. What could have happened during the night? I stood there totally stunned and in shock.

I managed to pull myself together and leave for the office. On the way out, I noticed Neal had stopped to speak to one of our neighbors. I drove on with my mind whirling as to Plan B, and I needed one very quickly.

That evening when I arrived back at the ranch, Neal told me the story of how our neighbor had neglected to close the gates on her horse pens, and during the night, the tulip- and pansy-eating monsters had visited my garden and helped themselves to "flower salad." She had retrieved the horses before I got up. I was not amused. But it was time for Plan B.

The day before the prom, I went to the nursery and bought flats of blooming flowers. I came home, planted them, and mulched so as to appear that they had been planted all season. I think I probably sat up all night looking out the window.

The next morning, all was well for prom photos and dinner. I, of course, took the compliments from parents and children as they photographed the couples with a stunning background of blooming flowers, wishing the whole time they could have seen the tulip-pansy extravaganza. Perhaps that is just like the "fish that got away" stories!

Every fall, I plant bulbs and plants with great hopes that a beautiful garden will be blooming in the spring. My lilies are new to the garden this year. And yes, I am already looking for new things to add this fall. *—May 2015*

Weed or Flower?

I finally have in captivity a Queen Anne's lace plant! I have been trying for years to get one to grow in my flower garden. I think it is one of the loveliest plants that grows in the South. It is just like looking at an intricate lace! Its blooms are used now in many wedding bouquets and arrangements, and it's just a beautiful accompaniment to larger flowers.

Weed or flower? I have thought about this many times: that what I see as a beautiful flower others see as a weed and vice versa. The same could be said of lantana. In South America, it is considered a weed, and here, we pay dearly for it for our gardens.

I know you have all seen the cute photo of a dandelion being blown into the wind. The caption reads, "A weed or 1,000 wishes?" It is all in the perspective, isn't it? I have always found eccentric people very intriguing. Many times, it's a person shunned by others because they are a little different whom I find fascinating. I can remember vividly a lady I met at the quilt market many years ago. She dressed in the most outlandish outfits. People loved seeing her, as she always had a story about her wardrobe. It was nothing for her to have a spray of flowers on her jacket with ribbons hanging out of every pocket. Some people would just laugh and walk away, but I just loved her commentary on life.

She was not old but old enough to have great experiences. She said that a person should never take themselves seriously. She had outlandish hats with birds on top and earrings dangling down to her shoulders, all of which she made herself. She spent hours making these masterpiece garments, and they were art creations.

I will never forget her excitement when she announced the engagement of her son to a lovely young lady. I asked her, "What are you going to wear to the wedding?" And she quickly replied, "Something just like I have on in hot pink." And you know me; I couldn't let that go, so I inquired if perhaps a more traditional mother-of-the-groom outfit might work better. She made the most profound statement and laughed: "Just what is a traditional mother of the groom? My son has never seen me dressed any other way and wouldn't know me!" Well, don't you know she was right! —*May 2018*

The Rose

Neal came inside from my garden and told me the most beautiful red rose was in full bloom. He planted this rose bush last year, and I really don't remember it blooming. I went out to see it and decided, since storms were forecasted, I would cut the flower to enjoy inside for the Easter weekend. The color was breathtaking.

Now, those of you who know me know I am not the biggest fan of red roses. My mother loves them, as this was the first flower my dad gave her when they were dating. For her, and everyone else in the world, they represent love. So, you are thinking—why does Phyllis not love red roses?

During my youth, red roses were the flower of choice when there were sad occasions. Funeral sprays, surgeries, and somber events. Yes, I know Valentine's Day is not sad, but my first glimmer as a child was this huge spray at my grandmother's funeral. Now I am talking about that black-red rose that was the order of the day. It's funny how we remember things like that from our childhood.

In my garden are many shades of pink, coral, and yellow roses, along with many other flowers that I adore. Each has its own personality and color, making each of them a star.

Back to this red rose. The color of this rose is vibrant, and the rose has a zillion petals. It's very different from those of my childhood. It was standing alone in the garden in all its glory when I brought it inside. As each day of the Easter weekend passed, I found myself really loving this fabulous rose. It almost became my symbol of hope for our country, as I watched the reports of the COVID-19 virus and the uncertainty people are facing everywhere.

Hope—that is what we must all continue to have. We must continue to hope that the cure will come quickly, that lives will be saved, that businesses will be protected so jobs will go on, that health care workers will have strength, and that families who have had loss will be comforted in some small way.

I thank God for the red rose Neal planted. The timing of the perfect bloom and the reminder of hope that it brought to me was treasured. Please have hope today. We are all struggling in many ways. We don't have answers or solutions, but hope will keep us going.

Love you all so much and know that we are all in this together. *—April 2020*

Why Monogramming Is Still My Go-to

Hobbies are amazing things. To quote one of my favorite sayings, "Why spend $2 on something when you can go to the crafts store, gather supplies, and make the same thing for $9?" There is some truth to that, isn't there?

I get lost in my hobbies. When I am in my sewing room, the world outside just passes me by. Time moves much quicker when I am making something. My passion is monogramming; I have this inner desire to monogram everything. I can hardly look at a garment without thinking about where I would put the monogram. Beautiful monogram designs naturally catch my eye.

At church on Sunday before the service started, this couple came in and introduced themselves, revealing that both their first names started with Rs as well as their last name. Without thinking or filtering my words, I blurted out, "Oh, my goodness, what an amazing monogram you have—three Rs!" The husband cocked his head and looked at me like I had four heads. He had no clue what I was talking about. She grinned and nodded with great delight!

It's funny, but when you adore monograms, nearly everything you see becomes a potential canvas for your next project. You rummage through antiques stores looking for "your letter," and goodness, if you find a set of napkins—the world stops spinning! The hunt is thrilling.

I love acorns and oak leaves. When Neal and I visited the Biltmore Estate, we realized throughout that magnificent house, acorns and oak leaves were imbedded in the architectural details. Some are carved in wood moldings, and others are chiseled into the exterior granite. The Vanderbilts, who built the home, loved the symbols, as the acorn and oak leaf represent strength and growth. Neal and I decided to incorporate acorns and oak leaves into the monogram we had designed after we married.

When we recovered our dining room chairs, we used the monogram motif, which was designed for us by artist Angela Atherton. I am amazed today at how many

times beautiful motifs show up in decorating, tableware, and textiles. For years, I have loved stitching the acorn motif into samplers.

These days, we are monogramming everything. Several of my friends have script monogram decals on the back windows of their cars. Young mothers today are laboring (no pun intended) over the initials that their soon-to-arrive babies will have.

What is it about monograms that we love so much? Well, the other day, I was reading a book about giving the perfect gifts, and the most amazing statement was there right in front of me: "When you give a monogrammed gift, the recipient knows that you planned ahead for the occasion." Oh, how true that is! *—April 2018*

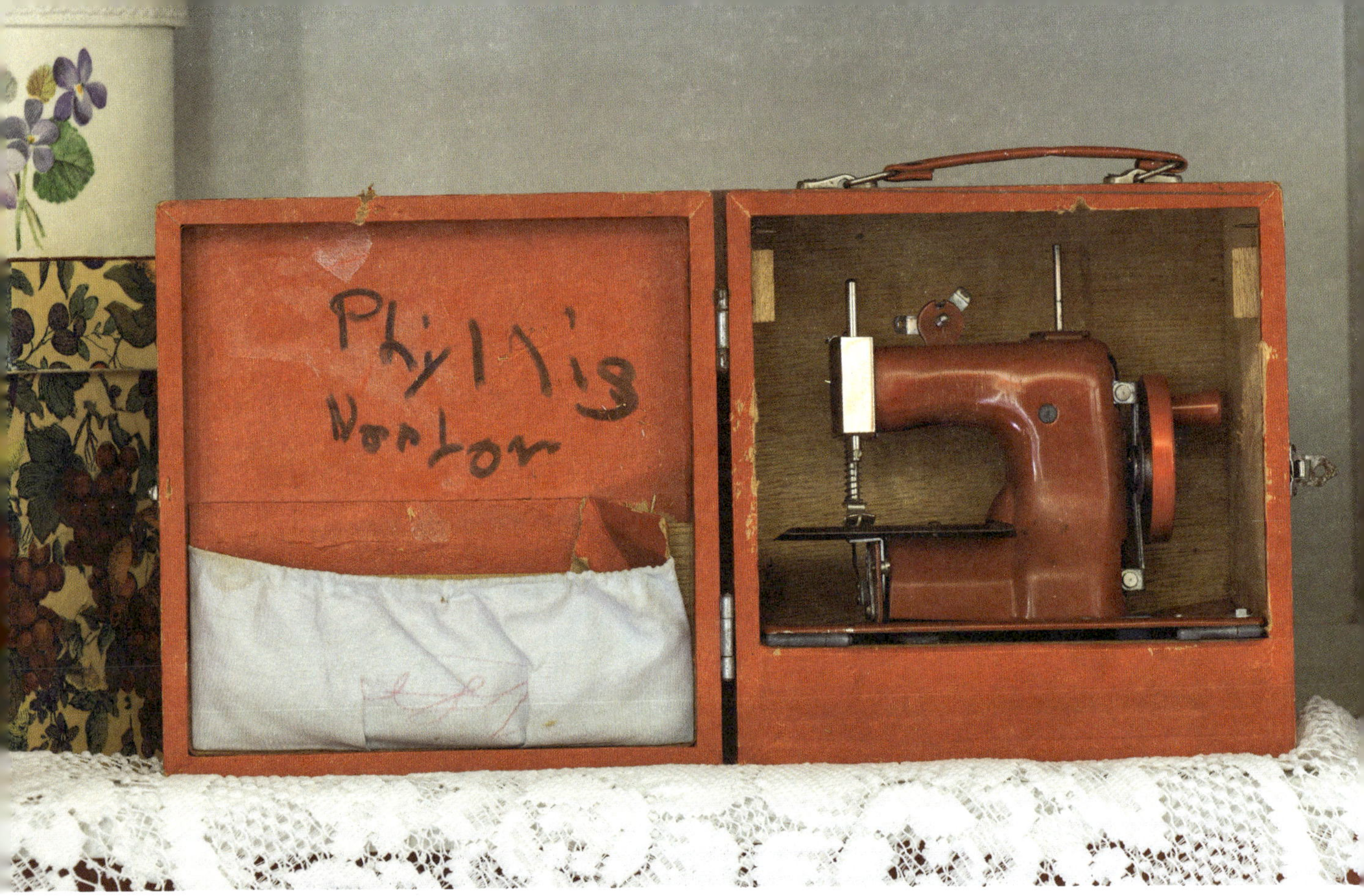

"Sewing is loving fabric; I can't seem to get enough. The other day I heard a perfect solution for those of us who tend to hoard; oh, I mean collect. Go through your collection of fabrics, stitching projects, and unfinished things, and put a tag on everything, making sure to name a family member. They will know you planned to make something for them."

Phyllis

Amelia Sewing

When my sweet little granddaughter, Amelia, told me that she wanted to learn to sew, my heart skipped a beat. She is almost 5 years old, so we will start with things she can do now. It will be a couple of years before she can operate a sewing machine. The journey of sewing together will begin soon.

I learned to sew when I was a little girl. Mom made our clothes, and it always intrigued me how fabric was cut, pinned, and sewn into a wonderful garment. Mom started me and my sister on simple things so we could become familiar with needles, threads, and working the machine. I've worked on samplers throughout my life.

My first sewing project was a hot pink apron complete with lace medallions stitched on top. I still have that apron and take great pride in the gathers of the skirt. I don't understand why I felt a cotton apron needed antique lace medallions, but who knows—embellishing is everything!

Step-by-step, you learn to sew. Many of you have shared your sewing stories with me. It is the love of fabrics and the process of assembling something that make sewing fun. I always looked forward to the day when I would sew for my children. I collected antique laces, ribbons, and buttons just waiting for that special little girl to come along. My twins were boys, my first grandchild was a boy, and then finally, there she was! Amelia would be the recipient of my labors. Thirty years I waited to use my treasures in creating beautiful dresses for her.

Amelia likes to play in my sewing room. When we are bored with the boy events at family gatherings, she always asks if we can go "fabric." That is her word for going to the sewing room, dragging out all of the fabric, and playing with patterns and color combinations. I just love it, and she is very good at coordinating colors!

As we begin our sewing journey, I look forward to the day when she will be able to make a garment on her own. It will be a day to remember. *—August 2015*

My Hand-Embroidered Tablecloth

Have you ever spent years on a project? The first time I undertook a long and difficult project was after I graduated from high school. My Grandmother Hill gave me some money as a graduation present because she knew that I wanted a tablecloth. The tablecloth that I wanted was not just any tablecloth. It was plain linen; however, it wouldn't stay that way for long. It came stamped with a border and center motif already on the cloth just ready for my eager fingers.

I love sewing and needlework, so my plan was to hand embroider the entire tablecloth. For as long as my 18-year-old self could remember, I had wanted to hand embroider a tablecloth all on my own. This was quite a lofty goal, and it took me several years to bring this project to completion. The finished product was a beautiful white linen embellished with taupe scrollwork. I even embroidered matching napkins to complement it. I was delighted to later find a gorgeous set of Lenox Lace Point dishes that matched the tablecloth. That pattern of dishes was only produced for two years, so they were quite a find. The tablecloth, napkins, and dishes all combined to make a tablescape that I am still proud of to this day. The process of embroidering took years, but I learned a lot about patience and discipline in order to complete the project.

If you have never undertaken an especially labor-intensive project, I highly recommend it. Though it may seem daunting at first, you are capable of far more than you think, once you discipline yourself. Even if it takes you years to complete, it will be worth it in the end. *—October 2016*

The Legacy of the Button Box

From the time of my earliest recollection, my mom had a button box. It was filled with every conceivable button that was made at the time. Buttons were never discarded and were reused on new garments when needed.

When my sister and I had a sick day from school—which meant we were close to death—we could play with Mom's button box. I would sort them by colors and sizes or just look through them time after time. What is it about button boxes that intrigue us? I recognized many of the buttons from dresses that had been worn out and shirts that my brother had worn until they were threadbare, but the buttons would live on in the box until needed again. The button box contains history.

I actually have two button boxes today—one for utilitarian purposes that contains all the spare buttons that come with ready-made garments and one for buttons that I have collected. The collectible buttons are from my grandmother's box, or they are special finds.

I have a pair of pearl buttons with the rhinestone centers that dates back to the 1700s and comes from an officer's uniform. I found these buttons several years ago at a wonderful little shop in New Orleans. Another find is a single button with an intricate design that I just love. I found this one at an antiques store and just had to have it.

Friends have given buttons to me, and I treasure them. One of my special button gifts was a delightful ring box made from an antique saltcellar. The lid is made of four buttons that are glued in a stack. The bottom button fits inside the glass cellar while the others are artistically stacked creating the handle. The top button is a shank rhinestone button that crowns the piece.

Several years ago, at a needlework trade show, I came across a mother-of-pearl button with the Christmas Nativity carved in the tiniest details. My heart stopped. This beautiful treasure was going home with me. It was glued to a black button and had a pin attached to wear as a brooch. The edges were chipped as the fragile button had many years of wear, but the beauty of this piece showed through. Later that year, another lady in the needlework industry started a business mounting buttons and pieces of china into silver findings. I took my prized little button to her and asked if it could be mounted securely into a sturdy mounting.

When I look at the tiny details of the carving, I am mesmerized every time as a new detail is discovered. The small star over the stable, the baby's halo, and the hands of Mary and Joseph are so intricate; I can't image the hours it must have taken to carve it. *—August 2014*

A Peek into My Sewing Tool Collection

I love to sew. It is through needlework and sewing crafts that Hoffman Media got its start. Over the years, I have collected untold numbers of sewing tools from chatelaines and pincushions to needle cases and thimbles.

When we launched the needlework publications in the 1980s, one of the most popular magazines was *Sampler & Antique Needlework Quarterly.* Inside those pages were patterns for sampler reproductions, historical information about needlework through the centuries, and fabulous collections of needlework and tools.

I have a few pieces left from my once-large antique sewing tool collection. The small acorns, both wooden and brass, are thimble cases. A woman would place her sewing thimble inside for safekeeping when not in use.

The barrel-shaped wooden case holds a tape measure that is hand-inked on a ribbon. If you needed to measure, you would pull it out and then rewind it by hand, turning the small spindle handle. In the spindle is a little round opening that contains a stanhope. This little optical device, introduced in the 1800s, contains images that can be seen by looking through the tiny lens. These were typical souvenirs of the day that are similar to small measuring tapes.

The two long rectangular flat, metal cases are for needles. These cherished needle cases held a woman's supply of sewing needles. These are great examples of the intricate metalwork that went into sewing implements. I also have a whole collection of antique scissors.

This is just a glimpse into the fascinating world of needlework tools. You probably have some treasured antiques in your sewing box—just take a look. *—August 2014*

The Pleasure of Baking

Do you love baking from scratch? I do. When I undertake a new baking project, I cherish getting out all of my "stuff" and laying out my pans, measuring cups, whisks, and measuring spoons. There's nothing quite like carefully adding each ingredient and ending up with a delicious result.

My grandkids know that when they come over, cookie baking is the order of the day. They know where everything is in the kitchen, and in years past, the first thing they would do was to pull out the step stool so they could reach the counter. Today, they are tall enough to reach, and the cookie tradition continues. When they were little, slice-and-bake would do the trick; now, the recipes have advanced a bit!

I learned baking at the knees of my mom and my grandmothers. I remember the whirl of my mom's mixer as the cake batter formed beautiful waves in the bowl. And who could forget the drama of whipped egg whites as they transformed into a perfect meringue?

I like to think my legacy lives through my sons, Eric and Brian, as both of them are accomplished cooks. Brian is editor of *Bake from Scratch* magazine, and Eric is masterful on a grill. We compare recipes and holiday menus, and I am somehow secretly pleased when they outdo me with theirs.

One of my favorite recipes developed by Brian are his biscuits. In the South, biscuits are a way of life. Born out of necessity and frugality, biscuits provided a high-calorie breakfast for those who worked a lot and did not have time to spend on meals. Now, these nostalgic and familiar staples are found in nearly every Southern restaurant and home kitchen and Southern buffet.

Nothing says Sunday in the South like covered-dish lunches at Grandmother's house. Some my favorite childhood memories are a table covered with a variety of dishes and baked goods. Pound cake was always involved, whether plain or a fancy caramel apple variation. I remember the tips my mother shared with me. The key is to make sure all your ingredients are at room temperature before you bake it. If the recipe calls for buttermilk, full-fat buttermilk is a must! Be sure to whisk your dry ingredients before adding them to your wet ingredients. And don't open the oven door until your cake has baked for most of the recommended time, or it may fall.

If you have been baking for years or just getting started on your journey, I wish you well and hope you find as much pleasure in it as I do. *—October 2018*

Miss Jo's Pound Cake

Around my house, everyone's favorite part of the meal is always dessert. I have always loved to bake with my family and especially love teaching my grandchildren how to bake. A simple and delicious recipe that is perfect for baking with children is Miss Jo's Whipping Cream Pound Cake. Miss Jo was a dear lady in my childhood church who was known as "The Pound Cake Lady."

Miss Jo always showed up with a fresh, warm pound cake at the most unexpected moments. She called it her pound cake ministry, and I thought that was the best! It was not uncommon for her to drop by our office when we were first getting started in our business and say, "I thought you girls just needed a pound cake today." And that simple gesture just changed our day. Her message was one of caring and brightening days. If Miss Jo knew you were going on vacation, she would pack a cake for you to take on your journey.

She passed away a few years ago. Her daughter and I grew up together, and when I asked about her story, Darlene told me that her mother made a pound cake every day for someone. Miss Jo set out her eggs and butter at night before she went to bed, and she was ready to go in the morning. I can't imagine how fabulous her kitchen must have smelled with its permanent pound cake fragrance!

This is one of the easiest cakes I have ever made, and it is always requested by my family. You can make individual cakes in ramekins, just adjust the cooking time. An ovenproof bowl is perfect to make a dome-shaped cake. Top it with a glaze, fresh fruit, or whipped cream. Not only is this treat wonderful to serve, but it makes me stop and think about Miss Jo. Her daughter was so wonderful to share this recipe.

Being known as The Pound Cake Lady is a wonderful legacy. As women, we create memories for our families and friends with acts of kindness. I wish I could hug Miss Jo and tell her how many lives she touched. She gave me a beautiful cut glass cake stand to use, and I think of her every time I use it. Bake a cake today . . . and share time with someone you love! *—October 2016*

JO'S WHIPPING CREAM POUND CAKE

Makes 1 (10-inch) cake

- 1 cup salted butter, room temperature
- 3 cups granulated sugar
- 5 large eggs, room temperature
- 3 cups bleached cake flour*
- 1 cup cold heavy whipping cream (not whipped)
- 1½ teaspoons vanilla extract

1. Preheat oven to 325°. Spray a 10-inch tube pan with baking spray with flour.

2. In the bowl of a stand mixer fitted with the paddle attachment, beat butter and sugar at medium speed until thoroughly combined, 1 to 2 minutes. Add eggs, one at a time, beating well after each addition. Reduce speed to low, and add flour and cream, alternately, scraping sides of bowl as needed. Add vanilla, increase speed to medium, and beat until light and fluffy, 3 to 4 minutes. Spoon into prepared pan, and spread even.

3. Bake until golden and a wooden pick inserted near the center comes out clean, 1 hour to 1 hour 10 minutes. Let cool in pan on wire rack for 30 minutes. Remove from pan, and let cool completely on wire rack.

**I use Swan's Down Cake Flour.*

Passion for Autumn

November has arrived with all the beauty of an autumn season. We usually don't get the gorgeous multicolored leaves until November here in Alabama. Some of you have had them for weeks in your area of the country. And some of you don't have any at all . . . beach friends! But this season is always special to me. It awakens the senses. It's an obsession.

Thanksgiving was always a special time for me growing up. The weeks leading up to the day meant thinking about the upcoming time of being with grandparents, aunts, uncles, and cousins. We always went to our grandparents' homes for that weekend. It was the custom in our family. Unless you were deathly sick, you didn't miss going. Family was important, and holidays celebrated family. The aunts all brought their favorite dishes, and Grandmother cooked her normal fare.

We girl cousins took our places on the porch, freezing to death but sharing stories of the current happenings in our lives. These memories are still very dear to me.

I loved hearing the stories of my parents' days when they were growing up and celebrating the holidays. I believe it is crucial to share stories from your life with children and grandchildren. Most of the time, they find things very strange compared to today, but they always ask questions. Sharing heritage is so important. I wish my grandparents were still around, as I have thought of a million things I would love to know about them. My mom still tells stories of her childhood, and I love that.

Are we sharing the things we should be with the young members of our family? As this crazy, fast-paced world whirls on, I want to spend time whenever we are together talking about moments in our lives. Times that helped shape us and taught us life's lessons. It also reminds us of the things that matter most in life. Time. Time that once passed cannot be relived.

Tell each child or grandchild about your feelings when they were born. Their faces glow when they hear how we loved them instantly. Remind them of the importance of family gatherings. And above all, tell them how much you love them. *—November 2021*

My Cake Stand Collection

Do you remember seeing a dish for the first time and instantly falling in love with it? I vividly remember one such experience that I had when I first saw my mother's cake stands. She had several that were all beautiful in their own way, but the one that instantly caught my eye was her Fostoria cake stand. I am lucky that my mother has gifted me this specific cake stand so that, as she said, I can make cakes for her now! Another one of my favorites has intricate etching all over, with three dainty birds carved into it. It truly is a timeless piece.

After my mother introduced me to cake stands, I began to build my own collection. Throughout the years, I have amassed many cake stands, each with their own unique charm.

My collection contains some old and some new, but each one carries its own special meaning. One of my more recent acquisitions is this white stand accented with metallic acorns. When my husband, Neal, and I got married, we adopted acorns as the symbol for our family. As emblems of growth, acorns are a motif that is carried throughout our home in various ways. This cake stand is one of my favorite ways that we incorporated acorns into our décor.

There is a cake stand for every season and occasion. Crystal stands are perfect for formal occasions, while basic stands can be used for everyday baking. An endless variety of cake stands is available in every style and price range. Starting a collection is a wonderful way to carry on a family legacy and pass a love of baking through the generations. *—August 2016*

Meet Author Alexandra Stoddard

I have been an Alexandra Stoddard fan since my friend Barbara Cockerham and I found a copy of her book *Living a Beautiful Life* in a bookstore in Williamsburg, Virginia. Barbara and I have a custom when we travel together of sitting at the end of the day with a cup of tea and reading aloud from a magazine or book. We call this time our daily "poetic reading." On that long-ago December evening, we fell under the spell of Alexandra's work.

In pondering the name for my blog, I recalled meeting Alexandra 10 years ago at a book signing. Inscribing her signature in my newly purchased copy of *Things I Want My Daughters to Know*, she placed a length of ribbon in its pages as her special way of adding a "grace note" to the moment. I named my blog as a tribute to Alexandra and the gracious lifestyle she promotes through the 28 books she has published. Alexandra and I have been friends since that day, and in 2008, she served as Writer-in-Residence for *Victoria* magazine.

Alexandra has spent her life helping others understand the path to true happiness. An interior designer by training, she credits Mrs. Eleanor McMillen Brown, her mentor, with her ability to shape spaces that allow homeowners to thrive in their own environment. I feel she has brought us an awareness of our surroundings and has encouraged us to find pleasure in detail. The design of her small volumes speaks to the feminine spirit. For those who experience delight through touch, her books are an experience in luxury. The velvety paper, the tinted ink, and the practice of including her endearing "grace notes," all combine to create a sense of bliss.

As a result of her writings, she has made us aware of the beautiful things we have in our lives rather than focusing on the things we don't have. She has helped us become mindful of the length of our days and has taught us to maximize the joy that we fill those days with, even when things in our lives might be challenging. She seeks beauty in the world, even in small measure. I recall that she wrote in one book of painting a band of color inside her kitchen cabinet doors, so that when she opens a cabinet, she is greeted with a bit of brightness that lifts her spirits. After hearing her describe her all-white writing room with a wooden desk, I want to go there for a visit and experience its splendor. Alexandra's view out the light-filled front window is of her gardens where beautiful French hydrangeas bloom.

She prides herself on writing on French paper with fountain pens rather than opting for a computer. "I love the sight of ink flowing and the sound of the pen as it moves across the paper, plus I have beautiful handwriting. The sunlight drenching the room gives me great energy as I write," she explains. One of my favorite books of hers is *Gift of a Letter*. For it is with our written words that we create a legacy of our thoughts and gratitude between family and friends. Thank you, Alexandra, for inspiring us to celebrate the joy of each day. *—May 2014*

How I Came to Love Tea

I have always admired and adored all things British. When Lady Diana became a household name and her wardrobe shaped the apparel business worldwide, I just loved it. My friend Barbara Cockerham and I actually studied her wardrobe and would buy every book we could find that had Diana as the subject.

One of the things we really loved and decided to master was the British ritual of having tea. Now mind you, we had no clue about tea blends, scones and curds, or any tea treat that one would typically make to accompany tea. We went to the store, bought shortbread cookies and lemon curd, and proceeded on to purchase Prince of Wales Tea.

When we finally got out our teapots and china cups, we thought we could pass for the royal family! But the truth is that basic tea started us both on a lifetime of loving tea and the wonderful foods that accompany tea. My favorite blend of tea is Earl Grey. It is a wonderful black tea that is steeped and then sipped to my extreme satisfaction. Nothing is as wonderful as a freshly baked scone with lemon curd and Devonshire cream.

Now, we never miss a tearoom when we travel. No two are alike! Many of you experienced your first tea at a tearoom. The delight of a tearoom's atmosphere is that people are always gathered, conversing madly to the clink of the china. It is heaven!

I also sample many teas along with Lorna Reeves, the editor of our *TeaTime* magazine. I can't get enough of beautiful settings, glorious teapots, and delectable foods. Can a woman own too many teapots? Of course not. What is it about teatime that transports us to another place? I can drink coffee on the run, but my tea must be savored, slowly sipped from a china cup.

I hope you fall in love with tea as I have. Every time I enjoy a cup of tea, it makes me relax and relish the moment. *—August 2014*

The Royal Wedding

I love all things British and get a bit of a thrill following the royal family. One of our Ribbon friends asked for my take on Prince Harry's upcoming wedding. That is such an interesting question, and you know me, I always have comments.

I am always pleased when two people who are in love decide to get married. I have watched Harry grow up through the years and finally make plans to settle down. Although, I am not sure getting married is settling down when you are in the royal family. When the eyes of the world are on their every move, a wedding just enhances the public interest surrounding Harry and his bride-to-be, American actress Meghan Markle.

It is no secret I loved Princess Diana and her spectacular matrimonial service. She and Charles got married the summer after my twins were born. As I was up around the clock with them, I watched the replay of the royal wedding a zillion times. I truly loved the ceremony, as I had never seen anything like it in my life. But really, aren't we all royal brides when we get married?

Princess Diana's choice of clothes, hats, shoes, and accessories revived an entire fashion industry in Britain. How refreshing to see her grow from kindergarten teacher's assistant to princess in just a few short months. Forget all the turbulent mess—I wish we could have seen her grow old with us. What a treat that would have been! But she is frozen in time as a beautiful young person—forever young, much like James Dean, Grace Kelly, and John F. Kennedy Jr.

Kate Middleton was a breath of fresh air when she and William got married. She knows her prince is in love with her and that shows on her beautiful face. Her style is one to be admired and copied as well.

Now, Harry and Meghan . . . what do I think of this? I think they are a cute couple, and they have an extreme opportunity to have a great influence on the young people of Britain. I am thrilled to see he is a patron to many wonderful charities and participates in multiple endeavors to benefit underprivileged people. They are sure of themselves and seem extraordinarily happy.

Like all women, I can't wait to see her dress, her flowers, her wedding party, and the parade of guests wearing hats to their wedding. In order to watch the televised event in a faraway time zone, I will be getting up before dawn to tune in and will sip tea and eat scones in the dark.

I don't know why, but the history and ceremonies of the British royal family fascinate me. It's a world I will never live in, and frankly, I wouldn't want to. I wish Prince Harry and Meghan all the best in their marriage and great happiness for the rest of their lives. *—January 2018*

The Royal Wedding in Review

I have looked at almost every photo that has been released, watched every piece of film, and read every commentary for which I had time. Summary: splendid.

I have asked myself a million times why I love the royal weddings, and I have come to this conclusion—all of us girls of the boomer generation were raised on Disney movies, back when they were all about good, and we loved the final scene of the movie when the couple gets married, dances, and lives happily ever after. We just love a good princess story, when dreams come true.

Maybe that is simplifying it a bit, but it is an escape into the world of beauty and love. I loved many things about this wedding, and they probably are not the obvious things you would think of. I think Prince Harry is adorable. He was just Harry and smiled from deep within. When he looked at his bride, his face said everything. She returned those loving glances and was just radiant.

I also loved the fact that Harry picked her flowers from the Princess Diana Memorial Garden at Kensington Palace. What a thoughtful thing to do. I have been through the garden, and it is breathtaking. He included his mother in subtle ways.

Meghan's dress was stunning. I have read many fashion commentaries about the dress, ranging from too simple and plain to perfection. I tend toward perfection. The mother of the bride had a beautiful coat-and-dress ensemble. Being the sewist that I am, I always look for amazing outfits. Did you see the embroidery on her coat? She had the perfect outfit for the day.

I can't help but admire Queen Elizabeth II for her impeccable taste and style. Her outfit was stunning. We all were still wondering what is in the queen's purse, but alas, someone solved it for us: extra hosiery! That makes sense, although I doubt she could disappear long enough to change.

All in, it was the perfect blending of the young couple. The sermon and the music were uplifting for all of us. We should all be encouraged that the world stopped that day, heard a sermon on loving our neighbors as ourselves, and witnessed the uniting of a young couple who just might change a little bit of the world we live in today. I wish them all happiness, joy, and a lifetime of love. Thank you for bringing your joy to all of us. —*May 2018*

"The sophistication of British life swooned me from an early age, and my dream of visiting this splendid country came true when I was 40 years old. From its picturesque streets to magnificent cathedrals, I could visit once a year and never grow tired of England!"

Phyllis

Exploring European Style

The Norton family, of which I am a descendant, came to America from England. In fact, when we were publishing needlework magazines, one of the great historians of needlework Joanne Harvey told me that she had created a needlework kit whereby I could recreate the Hannah Norton Alphabet Sampler from the Historic New England Collection. The original was stitched in 1795, and I am sure this is a direct link from me to some royal family in England—I just haven't figured it out yet.

All that to say, I love my English roots. I want my garden to look like an English cottage garden and my blue-and-white china collection to resemble those found in houses in Great Britain. Afternoon tea is a delight for me, and baking scones makes me feel a little more British. The first time I went to England, I loved the train rides through the countryside.

I felt the same when Neal and I traveled in France. What amazed me the most were the gardens that surround most every house in France. Gorgeous roses graced every yard and covered beautiful fences and walls. And if there is no garden, pots and planters filled to the brim with a breathtaking array of flora sufficiently fill the gap.

From luxurious castles to quaint farmhouses and charming villas, each kind of French home is enchanting in its own way. There is a fairy-tale quality to every abode—I could truly get lost for hours simply strolling around gazing affectionately at each home. The exteriors are spectacular, but the interiors boast a glorious mixture of textiles in plaids, toiles, and floral prints that I cannot seem to get enough of!

And, my, oh my, how I enjoy the darling little shops brimming with stacks and stacks of the plushest threads I have ever felt—fabric remnants, quilts and blankets, place mats and tablecloths—be still my linen-loving heart!

As with anything, we take bits and pieces of our travel experiences and incorporate them into our homes and gardens. I am holding on to a vintage blue-and-white linen from France that I can't decide what to do with. Until I make up my mind, I will keep admiring and refolding it over and over again. I may just need another piece to go with it. Thank goodness so many beautiful antiques have been imported into the US so that we can acquire wonderful pieces and add eclectic flair to our homes!
—August 2018

Montana

Neal and I just returned from a trip to Montana. We went there to escape the summer heat of Alabama only to find that we had taken the extreme heat with us. Everywhere we went, the locals kept telling us, "It is never this hot here." Such is our luck. We still had a marvelous time exploring the area, though.

There is nothing that can describe the magnificent mountains and the rivers that undulate around the terrain. I loved watching people fly fish in the Gallatin River and the young people floating down the river on inner tubes. They were having such fun.

We took a day trip to Yellowstone National Park in Wyoming, where we were delighted to see Old Faithful shoot steam many feet into the air. Apparently, it is so regular you can almost set your watch by it. People were gathered by the hundreds every time it erupted.

We loved the wildlife; it was baby bison time. You really had to watch as people would slam on brakes and come to complete stops in the road whenever there was a bison sighting. The elk were beautiful and seemed to put on a good show for the tourists, especially when they were grazing right in the center of town. But there was a respect for the wildlife and their beauty—you just had to keep some distance between you and the animals.

In Bozeman, Montana, we found a cowboy steakhouse (which delighted Neal) and a lovely quilt shop (which stole my heart). We have made a pact to explore our country and really take in the beauty of the United States. If you have never traveled to the West, then you might want to consider taking a trip there. *—July 2015*

le bistro
bord de

End of Summer Vacation Inspiration

For my family, summertime is often a season of travel. Traveling is one of my favorite pastimes, and I have been very fortunate to visit many beautiful places.

One of my favorite places to vacation is Asheville, North Carolina, where I can wander the gardens of the gorgeous Biltmore Estate. Gardens, especially flowers, have always been a source of inspiration for me. But Neal and I visited Biltmore last month so that I could see the fashion exhibit that is on display throughout the house. I was working on a feature story for the next issue of *Classic Sewing* and wanted to see the re-creation of Cornelia Vanderbilt's incredible wedding dress.

As we were touring the home and the exhibits, I was not only drawn to the beautiful fashions but to the amazing floral arrangements featured in every room. The entry foyer of the house had a floral wedding cake display that greets every guest. As I wandered through the tour, I was inspired by the combination of colors that the floral artist had selected. Upon inquiry, I was told that every week the Biltmore florists place new displays in every room open to the public. Some are asymmetrical while others are very balanced. I was so excited to be close enough to appreciate the artistry of these designers.

Upon my return home, having seen the beautiful flowers and arrangements at the Biltmore encourages me to fill my house with fresh blooms. The vibrant colors of flowers are an easy way to bring new life to a space. *—August 2016*

A Favorite Destination: Williamsburg, Virginia

Each time I visit Williamsburg, Virginia, I marvel at its colonial charm. Many of you know that I am totally consumed with this town and the historical events that occurred there during the 1700s.

When I walk down the streets of Colonial Williamsburg and see the character reenactments, knowing the presentation is far better than conditions were back then, I wonder just how they survived during those times. I love the glamorized version in movies and in plays, but truth be known, it was difficult!

From a woman's perspective, being dressed in all the layers of clothing in a world without air-conditioning is beyond me. But when you don't know anything different, you are likely accustomed to the heat. In the winter, they could at least build fires to keep warm, but I daresay they were probably freezing during those months. When I stroll through the town, the little fence-lined gardens beckon me to stop. I think about the colonists growing food in a strange land and how medical care was scarce.

The American Revolution and, ultimately, the signing of the Declaration of Independence took an enormous amount of commitment—a total commitment—from resettled people of England. I can't even imagine the sacrifices that were made to form this country, our country.

Our country is still the place for me and Neal. May we always respect each other, love this country, and look for the good in the world around us.—*July 2018*

Dried Flowers

My first trip to Colonial Williamsburg was life-changing in many ways. In addition to the wonderful architecture and the enchanting furnishings, I discovered what the colonists called "everlastings." Everlastings are dried flowers placed in beautiful arrangements so that during the dreary winter months the memories of beautiful flowers can be preserved.

My mom, Inez Norton, is the queen of dried flowers. She always jokes and says you better look fast if you want to see the flowers in the garden; she will have them hanging to dry faster than you can blink. I asked her one time if larkspur is a reseeding plant. She laughed and said, "I have no idea. I pick the flowers before I give them time to reseed." She plants seeds every year just to be sure she has a beautiful bed of flowers.

Roses are so easy to dry. I hang mine upside down and just leave them alone. But I usually wait until right before the petals are ready to drop unless I want to preserve a rose in bud. All summer long, Mom and I both look for beautiful blossoms to dry; when we have enough (or the boxes are running over), Mom makes beautiful arrangements or refreshes older arrangements. Sometimes you just need to throw them away because they become so brittle they crumble.

I just love everlastings. There is something so elegant to me about dried flower arrangements. The colonists really knew how to bring beauty inside to enjoy long after growing season. While it is still winter, spring will be coming soon. You should think about drying some of your favorite flowers to enjoy next winter.
—February 2015

Christmas Destination: Williamsburg, Virginia

How I love Christmastime! We set aside time for the people, places, and moments that become part of our treasured holiday memories. For many of us, our Christmas travel traditions are abbreviated this year because of the pandemic. One of my usual trips is to Williamsburg, Virginia, to walk down Duke of Gloucester Street and admire the decorations, eat at a wonderful tavern, and do some shopping. This year, I will be staying home, but I wanted to share with you of one of my favorite places to go: Seasons of Williamsburg.

Seasons of Williamsburg, a premiere floral and giftware shop, has already decked the halls for the holidays, and owner Kendall Kirby kindly shared a sneak peek. It was his way of spreading holiday cheer. We have featured this exquisite shop in many of our magazines through the years, and going there has been a part of my holiday celebrations for years. I can't describe the overwhelming beauty that lies within these walls.

Each year, the offerings are completely different than the previous year. Each tree has unique ornaments and trims. This year, the shop has a stunning silver tree with blue-and-white ornaments, and I went nuts over it.

Kendall has become a cherished friend over the years, and when he sent me this preview, it lifted my spirits. If I can't be there, at least I got to see it in photos. Thank you, Kendall, for making our world beautiful every year. Christmas is magical at Seasons. —*November 2020*

GATE LEG TABLE
CHERRY
ALBEMARLE CO. VA

My Time in Alaska

Summer travel for me is escaping to a cooler climate. Don't get me wrong; I love the wonderful gardens and flowers of the South, but a respite from the heat can be restorative. Neal and I just love Alaska! If you haven't been, let me suggest taking a cruise through the glaciers. In our hurried world, this journey allows us to retreat to tranquility and to observe the pristine shores where glaciers touch the water.

I had heard about glaciers my whole life and never expected to see such a splendid sight. As the cruise ship moved into Glacier Bay, there was a hush of respect for the unblemished nature before us. We watched the wildlife move from the freezing blue-green waters onto icebergs to rest.

The cold air was refreshing and chilled us to the bone. When the glacier would break and a slice would fall into the water, a loud thundering sound would echo down the fjord. We stood in awe of the majesty of creation. The tiny fishing villages intrigued me as we passed by them. I wondered: "What must winter be like in this frozen country?"

One of our favorite things to do is to have coffee on the deck and watch the bald eagles soar. I've never really considered the vast size of these glorious birds. Oh, my! When the first one flew overhead, I could hardly believe it! The gorgeous evergreens seem to stand majestically at attention. I can only imagine the fragrance if you were lucky enough to walk through the "Christmas tree" forest. I never tire of the landscape. The splendor of whales jumping is a sight to behold.

I am most astonished by the glaciers. The rich turquoise color of the frozen fields is breathtaking. Seeing that makes me appreciate the greatness of God's creation. The waterways around the glaciers are sacred grounds, and they are kept with respect to the wildlife living there.

When Neal and I got married, we took all our children and grandchildren on this cruise to celebrate. Don't be afraid to bring children because even the youngest will adore this cruise. Everyone in our family came away with favorite experiences from salmon fishing to eating smoked salmon and local cuisine in the villages. Neal and I love to stroll and explore the beguiling little towns in Alaska. I always find quilt shops and buy fabric and yarns native to Alaska. What a treat!

I encourage you to visit this beautiful state. You will create memories that will last a lifetime. *—June 2016*

The Little Things

My love for writing comes as no surprise to you. From the special joy of writing with a classic cartridge pen to my thoughts on sending a meaningful thank-you note, I have shared with you more than once how much writing means to me. I've even shared my foray into calligraphy.

It appears that several of you share my sentiments. When I recently posted about how important it is to set aside time to write words of encouragement, a number of you shared how you love to keep stationery on hand for such occasions. One reader explained that she keeps a calendar marked with the special people in her life to whom she wants to take time to write. What a thoughtful way to keep yourself from neglecting loved ones in this busy world!

I think, as I grow older, I realize more and more the little things in life are the things that matter most. By this point in our lives, we've usually mastered the big picture, but it's focusing on the little details that make it a masterpiece.

Whether it's setting a beautiful table, monogramming pretty napkins, displaying a collection you love, or organizing treasured letters and notes you have saved for years—the things that give us great pleasure and bring happiness are the little things I am talking about, not only for ourselves but for others as well.

This year, I want to enjoy flowers inside and outside. There is nothing dreamier than having a blossom on my desk or on my side table at home. Last year for Christmas, I received a flower as a gift. Our editor of *TeaTime* magazine, Lorna Reeves, put one on my desk every week last year. I always looked forward to that, and it changed my outlook. How refreshing and how restorative it was to enjoy those beautiful blossoms.

I think it goes back to the time when my twins were young boys. They would pick weeds, flowers, leaves, and anything that looked like a bouquet to them and bring it inside to me. I had little vases lined up on my windowsill where I could enjoy each little item. Those little dirty hands would hold up a tightly clasped collection of their precious treasures, and we would put them in vases to display them. What joy!

It wasn't just the flowers; it was the reminder that they loved me and thought of me. Really that's all anyone wants to know, isn't it? How lovely it would be to brighten someone's day with something as simple as a flower. *—January 2018*

CREATIVITY AND LOVE

THE CHERISHED COLLECTIONS PHYLLIS enjoyed are a heartwarming testimony to a life of purpose, creativity, and boundless love. Her vibrant spirit and zest for life are reflected in her passions, from the intricate world of needle arts to the serene beauty of blue-and-white china. Each item in her collection tells a story—of cherished travels, nurtured gardens, and moments savored over a perfect cup of tea in a lovely teacup.

Phyllis deeply loved quilting, sewing, and embroidery, by hand and machine. My favorite memories are the times we shared in the sewing room. Oh, the stories, memories, and secrets we shared while sewing. When we entered the sewing room, we would leave the cares of the world behind to jump into making dresses for our granddaughters, altering a wedding dress or formal wear for friends, replacing missing buttons on shirts for one of the guys at the office or catching up on "fixing" holes and hems for family members. She always generously shared her sewing skills. If we made any sewing mistakes, Phyllis had a unique talent for turning them into something lighthearted and funny. To her, a mishap was simply a creative opportunity to make it right and move forward—this alone speaks volumes about how she lived her life.

Phyllis had an extraordinary gift for inspiring others. She believed in the creative potential of every person she met, always encouraging them to try new things and discover hidden talents. Her collection of antique buttons, embroidered postcards, and silver bells is not just about the objects themselves but the delight of discovery and the beauty of the little details. She was a truly remarkable woman who touched countless lives with passion, grace, faith, and unwavering kindness. —*Kathy McMakin, editorial director of* Classic Sewing

Kathy McMakin

Final Thoughts

BUTTERFLY SKY

THIS WAS INTENTIONALLY THE LAST PIECE written for this book because I wasn't sure that it should be included. But in the same way Mom opened her heart and thoughts to people through her blog, I want to do the same in hopes that it will help anyone facing grief and the loss of loved ones. Without sharing details that will forever remain private, you need to know that Mom passed away in Seattle, Washington, after her health began to fail while on a family vacation to celebrate her upcoming 70th birthday.

In the last few days of Mom's time with us, I knew I needed some minutes alone with her to pour my heart out and share my gratitude to her for being the best Mom in the world. I also held her hand and assured her that I would be OK . . . something I knew she needed to hear.

During that conversation, she turned her head to me and said, "Are we flying home?" To which, I replied, "Yes, Mom, we will fly home when you are better!" After thinking about it for a minute, she continued, "Can we go on a butterfly?" In that very second before replying, my eyes filled with tears. My heart knew that we were talking about flying home to different places. I grabbed her hand a little tighter and said, "That sounds like a perfect plan."

A few days later, on July 10, 2023, Mom went to eternal rest surrounded by her husband, sons, son-in-law, and her siblings. Since that day, butterflies have surrounded us. We see them when we need to feel her presence, on days when grief is heavy and debilitating, and at times when something needs to be celebrated.

The sky has always been home to me. My first career took me all over the world as a flight attendant, and travel remains one of my biggest passions. It was very fitting that the first butterfly I saw the week of Mom's passing was in the clouds. Stephen and I were sitting on our balcony overlooking our home city of Birmingham,

Alabama, when I looked up through tear-filled eyes and saw clouds forming a butterfly in one of the most beautiful sunsets that I've ever seen. In that moment, I knew Mom was showing herself to me through a butterfly sky. I looked up and said, "Hey, Mom. I miss you, and I love you so much."

Grief has been the hardest thing I've ever dealt with in my life. I've learned a few things along this journey that I want to share with you. If you are grieving, don't suppress it. Be in it. Feel it. It was shared with me that tears are simply an expression of love that has nowhere else to go. Eventually, strength returns. Mourning will fade, but grief will last a lifetime as you move forward in honoring the life of your loved one.
—Brian Hart Hoffman

I wish you wondrous things
that can't be tied up
in ribbons and bows.
I wish you thoughts that take
you to magnificent places.
I wish you togetherness and
abundant happiness.
And, I wish you quiet times
all to yourself, when the grace
of all that is good in your life is
sweetly celebrated within.

Epilogue: On Grieving

I have been sitting here reflecting on the events of the past three weeks and wondering, what do you say? My dad passed away a couple of weeks ago. It was life-changing for our family, but we know he is in Heaven, pain free, and happy. We know that in our minds, and we just need our hearts to catch up.

I have learned so many things through this time that I wanted to share with you. The overwhelming outpouring of love and concern has touched our lives. People that we have known from our past, people we work with, and our friends and family have reached out to us, and it really meant so much.

There have been times I should have called or written a card when people were grieving, but didn't as I got distracted and excused it away. To the hundreds of people who reached out to us, thank you for showing me it matters. Every note, email, and call makes such a difference.

Life is meant to be lived. My dad lived life to the fullest. We have laughed at his coupons that were left where he fully intended to "get a bargain." We have shared stories with people, and they have shared with us. Talking and laughing is very healthy for all. Each one who shared with us told of their experiences with Dad—many we knew, and others we just heard for the first time. How fabulous it was to talk. Don't be afraid to talk with people grieving. It is really very restorative to the soul.

I have shared many stories with you on Ribbon about Mom and Dad. We learn from people in our lives, and they are always our best teachers. God puts people in our lives for a reason. I am the firstborn of the three children. You have heard from my sister, Janice, on Ribbon and my brother, Keith, is hoping I never write about him—all in fun. Although he says he should write about both me and Janice . . . we'll see. We are blessed to have great parents who realized that we are individuals and unique. That's what makes families! All the various personalities blended into one household but each remaining as an individual. They never tried to make us into someone we were not intended to be. They let us be ourselves and encouraged us to develop our own interests and talents.

Grieving is an individual thing. Everyone grieves in their own way. I have observed this during this time, and it is so true. And we must always give ourselves permission to grieve. It is a part of life and a part of who we are.

Many of you have reached out to me during this time, and I am forever grateful. I love our Ribbon group, and I know that together we make a difference! Much love to you all. —*October 2018*

(Opposite) Poem I read at Mom's funeral. —Brian

Her Last Post: Dear Friends

I am sitting at my desk overlooking my flower garden right outside the window. I concluded that flowers make summer endurable. The heat in the South can get to you, but the dewdrops on flower petals seem to calm everything. We all like certain parts of every season, but we have our favorite.

That's the way life is. Certain parts we love more than others. We must find the good in all parts. That's hard to do sometimes. When there is sickness, loss, or discouragement, it seems impossible at times. But my plan is to find something wonderful each day and dwell on it for a while. Today, it's the bright yellow calla lilies, red lilies, and roses.

I find it fascinating that every winter these flowers go to sleep and rest. When those first warm rays hit the garden, up they come. Each year, they multiply and bring more blossoms to enjoy. I have an emotional attachment to several flowers. My brother brought me a beautiful pink lily, and every year, it amazes me with its beauty. It's in bud now and will be blooming soon. My grandson loves lamb's ears, the soft gray plant that multiplies also. It feels like fur.

So, you are asking, what does all this have to do with life? We must make it a habit to look for the good around us every day. Find one thing that makes you smile and dwell on it. Dwelling on something causes us to slow down, ponder, and spend time resetting our outlook. It's hard today with the uncertainty around us.

My mom reminded me years ago that flower bulbs and cuttings were shared with friends. During the Great Depression, no one had money for flowers, but some of the most beautiful gardens bloomed during that time. They concentrated on sharing beauty with others. I have flowers in my garden from my grandmother's garden. Sharing beauty continues.

Today, I hope you find a beautiful moment to enjoy. Thank you all for the prayers and emails from you that bring beauty to me. Have a blessed day. *—June 2023*

"I am thankful for so many things and thank God for his many blessings. My family has always been the most important gift for which I am thankful."

Phyllis

AFTERWORD

AS I WRITE THESE WORDS, I AM FILLED WITH A DEEP sense of reverence and love for my sister, Phyllis. It was an immense privilege to be her brother. When her sons, Brian and Eric, asked me to contribute to this book, *The Ribbon in Her Journal*, I felt both honored and humbled to share my reflections on her life and her work.

Phyllis was not only my sister but also a guiding light in my life. From a young age, she exhibited a remarkable ability to capture the world around her through many talents. Phyllis was the smartest, most gifted person I have ever known. She was a certified public accountant, an entrepreneur, an artist, a seamstress, an author, a great cook, and, to top it all off, an extremely talented pianist and organist. Her talent as a publisher and writer was only matched by her compassion and understanding of others. *The Ribbon in My Journal* blog was her way of weaving her experiences, thoughts, and emotions into a tapestry that resonated with others.

Growing up with Phyllis, I witnessed firsthand her dedication to anything she attempted to master. She was meticulous, always striving for perfection, yet she lived life with a raw honesty that drew people in. Her journal was more than just a collection of articles; it was an intimate glimpse into her heart and soul. Through her writing, she shared her joys, her struggles, and her innermost thoughts, creating a profound connection with her readers.

The transformation of *The Ribbon in My Journal* into *The Ribbon in Her Journal* is a testament to her enduring impact. Brian and Eric have lovingly compiled her writings, preserved her voice, and ensured that her legacy continues. This book is a celebration of Phyllis—her life, her passion, and her unwavering spirit.

I would like to extend my deepest gratitude to everyone who has supported this project. To Phyllis's sons, thank you for your dedication in bringing this book to life. To the readers, thank you for taking the time to engage with her words. Your support means more than words can express.

As we turn these pages, let us remember the ribbon that binds us all—love, resilience, gratefulness, and the shared passion that Phyllis had for all of us who knew her. My sister's journey was unique, yet her reflections touch upon universal truths that we can all relate to. Her words remind us to cherish every moment, to embrace our vulnerabilities, and to find strength in our connections with one another.

Thank you, Phyllis, for opening your heart and sharing your story with us. Your legacy lives on through these pages, and your spirit continues to inspire. You are deeply missed, but your light will never fade. *—Keith Norton, brother*

Journaling Tips

To Help You Get Started

1 FIND A PLACE AND GATHER YOUR TOOLS.
First, you must find a comfortable spot to write. It could be a desk, a nook in your home, or even the kitchen table. Select your writing instrument and paper or journal. A lovely pen and nice paper can add to the pleasure of keeping a journal.

2 SET A TIME.
Choose a day or two each week that you will commit to writing. Don't skip it.

3 THINK BEFORE YOU WRITE.
Once you have a time and place, sit and ponder for a minute. Let your thoughts go. You can choose a topic or just write freely about what you are thinking. Keep it private as this is your personal moment, and it's important to be honest. Express all the things you don't want to say aloud.

4 KEEP A LIST OF PROMPTS.
Make a list for the days when you have trouble coming up with something to write. One word can often inspire you; for instance, include topics like planning, prayer, gratitude, sorrow, hope, dreams, or love. Or create a list of questions: What about family? Where do I want to travel? What happened today? Greatest regret? Happiest days?

Friendship is born
at that moment when

5 GIVE EACH ENTRY A TITLE AND DATE.

The date organizes your journal. Adding a phrase will help you in the future when you reread your feelings. Putting a short headline can help you understand your thoughts and actions in certain situations and give you inspiration or reassurance at difficult times.

6 WRITE LOOSELY AND WITHOUT RESTRAINT.

Don't worry about order, sentence structure, grammar, spelling, or punctuation. Just put down on paper what is in your head. Let it flow honestly and naturally.

7 ENJOY THE MOMENT.

Writing in a journal should be fun. Make yourself laugh. You should derive pleasure from journaling. The process should be cathartic and renew your spirit.

Phyllis's first painting.

ACKNOWLEDGMENTS

To our mom, who surrounded us with love and will eternally do so from her place of rest. All of this is possible because of you. Your life was about giving and caring for others. How fortunate are we that we got to call you Mom?!

To Neal, Phyllis's husband, for selflessly giving up so much to care for Mom as she battled medical obstacles in her final years. She loved you so much, and the adventure of your love story took her out of her comfort zone and was the thrill of her lifetime.

To our Aunt Janice and Uncle Keith, Phyllis's siblings, thank you for filling in the gaps with stories and photos of Mom's childhood. We are so grateful Mom had siblings that loved her so much and surrounded her in her final moments before entering eternal rest.

To our spouses, Katie (Eric) and Stephen (Brian), we are grateful to you for being our rock of support during our grief. Losing our mom, boss, and business partner upended our lives, and your support through all of it has been needed and appreciated. She loved both of you as her own.

To Hays and Amelia, thank you for loving your Gigi so much. From daily FaceTimes with Hays to share his hunting and fishing stories to countless afternoon teas and spa days with Amelia—and so many other fun adventures—your love for Gigi made her days better. We now understand why our Mimi, Phyllis's mom, said, "If I knew how amazing it was to be a grandmother, I would have done that first!" Being Gigi was bliss for Phyllis.

To Lorna Reeves, our sister and colleague, as well as a source of strength and steadiness for so many years. You were a part of our family from the time we were toddlers. We took you in as "sissy" just as quickly as Mom took you as one of her own. You never missed a chance to share compassion and love with Mom, and for that we can't thank you enough.

To our team at Hoffman Media, you are the best in our industry, and we are so fortunate to be your colleagues. Your fast action to surround us in the days after Mom passed away and keep the company running, without missing one deadline or detail, speaks to the level of talent and passion you bring to the company. Not only were you mourning the loss of our leader, but you stepped up in the gap of our sorrow to allow us to grieve our mom, and for that we are forever grateful.

To Brooke Bell, Marie Baxley, Tracy Wood-Franklin, Stephanie Welbourne-Steele, and Melissa Sturdivant Smith—the dream team of this book project. Thank you for honoring our mom and shaping this book to convey her spirit. Because of this book, we have a printed tribute to our hero. She will continue to inspire others through her life and shared words.

—Brian and Eric